Series/Number 07-143

D0076205

MULTILEVEL MODELING

DOUGLAS A. LUKE
Saint Louis University School of Public Health

SAGE PUBLICATIONS
International Education and Professional Publisher
Thousand Oaks London New Delhi

For information:

Sage Publications, Inc.
2455 Teller Road
Thousand Oaks, California 91320
E-mail: order@sagepub.com

Sage Publications Ltd.
1 Oliver's Yard
55 City Road
London EC1Y 1SP
United Kingdom

Sage Publications India Pvt. Ltd.
B-42, Panchsheel Enclave
Post Box 4109
New Delhi 110-017 India

Printed in the United States of America on acid-free paper.

Library of Congress Cataloging-in-Publication Data

Luke, Douglas A.
    Multilevel modeling / Douglas A. Luke.
        p. cm.—(A Sage university papers series. Quantitative applications in the social sciences ; 143)
Includes bibliographical references.
ISBN 978-0-7619-2879-9 (pbk)
    1. Multivariate analysis. 2. Multilevel models (Statistics) I. Title. II. Series.
QA278.L85 2004
519.5′35—dc22   2003027811

    11 12 13 14   11 10 9 8 7

Acquiring Editor:	Lisa Cuevas Shaw
Editorial Assistant:	Margo Crouppen
Project Editor:	Claudia A. Hoffman
Copy Editor:	Liann Lech
Typesetter:	C&M Digitals (P) Ltd.

ACKNOWLEDGMENTS

Early versions of this monograph were presented to a group of colleagues and students at Saint Louis University participating in an independent study project on multilevel techniques. I would like to thank Missy Kraus, Sarah Boslaugh, Tegan Boehmer, Christy Hoehner, and Mike Elliott for their challenging questions and helpful comments. In particular, I would like to thank Missy Krauss for her early work with me on the tobacco voting project—her hard work and insights helped shape my thinking about the applicability of multilevel models. Finally, I would like to dedicate this book to my first teachers: Robert and Susan Luke.

CONTENTS

SERIES EDITOR'S INTRODUCTION

In the modeling of human behavior, context can be terribly important. Individual action may be determined by independent variables operating at different levels, from the micro to the macro. For example, the campaign dollars that a voter contributes to a candidate could be a function of individual characteristics (e.g., the voter's income and education) and group characteristics (e.g., the voter's neighborhood or professional associations). Given these possible effects from different levels, the researcher might estimate an ordinary least squares (OLS) regression model, $V = a + bI + cS + dN + eP + u$, where V, I, and S = individual-level measures on contributions, income, and education, respectively; N and P = group-level measures of the neighborhood and the professional association, respectively; b and c = parameters of individual effects; d and e = parameters of contextual effects; and u = error. Such an approach can be useful, and is explicated in an earlier monograph in the series by Iversen, *Contextual Analysis,* No. 81.

But, in the presence of multilevel effects, it can be difficult for OLS to meet the classical regression assumptions. In particular, having individuals in the same group will likely lead to violation of the assumption of uncorrelated errors. This circumstance, which is fully treated here, requires multilevel modeling with maximum likelihood estimation (MLE). Multilevel models are sometimes called other things—hierarchical linear models, random coefficients models, mixed effects models—and the approach may be single equation- or simultaneous-equations. The focus of Dr. Luke is on single-equation, regression-style, two-or three-level modeling. He uses very effectively the example of pro-tobacco voting by members of Congress as a function of individual-level (e.g., PAC contributions) and aggregate-level (e.g., the home state) characteristics, offering an MLE of effects from the two levels, and providing an excellent discussion of goodness-of-fit measures— deviance, Akaike Information Criterion (AIC), and Bayesian Information Criterion (BIC).

Various extensions of the technique are provided. For instance, the use of generalized hierarchical linear models (GHLM) for estimation in the case of discrete or non-normal dependent variables is offered. Furthermore, there is discussion of longitudinal data where time is nested within person, as in a health survey panel with respondents interviewed multiple times and having considerable variability in their missing data. Such a condition is difficult to treat with the standard repeated-measures MANOVA, but it can be handled with multilevel modeling. Also, the autocorrelation problem, typical of longitudinal data, receives explication. In the field of multilevel modeling, issues of design and analysis are rapidly evolving, which makes for much new and changing software. Fortunately, then, Dr. Luke provides a detailed look at two popular packages—HLM and R/S-Plus—and provides a table and discussion of more specialized programs, including those in SAS and SPSS. For researchers who want a sophisticated discussion of multilevel models in plain language, this is their monograph.

—*Michael S. Lewis-Beck*

Series Editor

MULTILEVEL MODELING

DOUGLAS A. LUKE

Saint Louis University School of Public Health

I should venture to assert that the most pervasive fallacy of philosophic thinking goes back to neglect of context.

John Dewey, 1931

1. THE NEED FOR MULTILEVEL MODELING

When one considers almost any phenomenon of interest to social and health scientists, it is hard to overestimate the importance of context. For example, we know that the likelihood of developing depression is influenced by social and environmental stressors. The psychoactive effects of drugs can vary based on the social frame of the user. Early childhood development is strongly influenced by a whole host of environmental conditions: diet, amount of stimulation in the environment, presence of environmental pollutants, quality of relationship with mother, and so on. The probability of teenagers engaging in risky behavior is related to being involved in structured activities with adult involvement. A child's educational achievement is strongly affected by classroom, school, and school system characteristics.

These examples can be extended to situations beyond where individuals are being influenced by their contexts. The likelihood of couples avoiding divorce is strongly related to certain types of religious and cultural backgrounds. Group decision-making processes can be influenced by organizational climate. Hospital profitability is strongly affected by reimbursement policies set by parent HMOs.

What all of these examples have in common is that characteristics or processes occurring at a higher level of analysis are influencing characteristics or processes at a lower level. Constructs are defined at different levels, and the hypothesized relations between these constructs operate across different levels. These types of "multilevel" theoretical constructs

1

require specialized analytic tools to properly evaluate. These multilevel tools are the subject of this book.

Despite the importance of context, throughout much of the history of the health and social sciences, investigators have tended to use analytic tools that could not handle these types of multilevel data and theories. In earlier years, this was due to the lack of such tools. However, even after the advent of more sophisticated multilevel modeling approaches, practitioners have continued to use more simplistic single-level techniques. Why has this been the case? A number of epistemological traditions have shaped this behavior. First is the long reach of the positivist tradition. Even many years after philosophers of science have established the inadequacy of logical positivism as a framework for the biological, health, and social sciences, we still tend to emphasize research designs and analytic tools that trace their roots back to a positivist stance. For example, the emphasis on control over experimental and observational conditions, the reliance on control and comparison groups, and the use of modeling techniques that statistically "remove" or control for the effects of covariates all combine to provide a lot of precision over inferences. However, at the same time, they severely restrict the ability to measure or evaluate extra-individual, contextual effects.

Another aspect of positivism is that it is most effective at describing sciences that deal predominately with closed systems. The behavior of closed systems, such as the movement of planetary bodies, can be predicted based on knowledge of only a few variables, such as mass and velocity. The social and health sciences, on the other hand, deal with much more complex open systems (Bhaskar, 1989). With open systems, by definition, it is impossible to control, restrict, or remove the effects of outside contextual influences. Thus, it becomes important to be able to adequately measure and analyze those effects, using appropriate multilevel methods.

A second example is how the medical model has shaped much of our research. The medical model takes a reductionist view of health: Disease is seen simply as a defect in the person that is corrected by medical intervention. We can see how this plays out, for example, in how modern epidemiologists identify risk factors for disease. Epidemiology has constructed a number of powerful design approaches (e.g., case-control studies) and analytic tools (e.g., logistic regression that produces relative risk estimates) that are used to identify significant risk factors for development of, say, cardio-vascular disease. Important risk factors for CVD include genetic predisposition; biology (high blood pressure); behavior (smoking, exercise); culture (ethnicity); and environment (access to health care). However, even though these factors clearly are operating at different levels, they are almost always measured at the individual-level (through surveys, for example), and little attention is paid to the mechanisms by which these factors operate. For example, is lack of exercise an individual issue of personal choice, or is it an ecological issue of lack of access to opportunities for physical activity in the immediate neighborhood?

Despite what the above critique suggests, there has been increasing interest and activity in promoting a more multilevel approach in the behavioral, health, and social sciences. One very prominent example is the 2000 report issued by the National Institutes of Health (NIH), entitled *Toward Higher Levels of Analysis: Progress and Promise in Research on Social and Cultural Dimensions of Health* (Office of Behavioral and Social Sciences Research, 2000). This report presented a new agenda for NIH research focusing on two goals: (a) expanding health-related social sciences research at NIH, and (b) integrating social science research into interdisciplinary, multilevel studies of health. For the purposes of this monograph, the most relevant recommendation of the report was to:

... support the development of state-of-the-art social science methods. Challenges include measurement at the group, network, neighborhood, and community levels; the further development of methods for longitudinal research; multi-level research designs that integrate diverse qualitative and quantitative approaches ...; and the development of improved methods for data collection and analysis. (p. 3)

Table 1.1 presents a conceptual framework based on the NIH report for understanding the interdependence among levels of analysis, here with an example from the area of tobacco control. Research programs on tobacco control exist at all levels of analysis, from the genetic up to the sociocultural and political. Moreover, although research can occur strictly within any of these levels, much of the most important research will look at the links between the levels. For example, as we learn more about the genetic basis of nicotine dependence, we may be able to tailor specific preventive interventions to particular genotypes.

We can see the interdependent and hierarchical nature of these multilevel influences on health more clearly from another national initiative: the 2003

4

TABLE 1.1
Levels of Analysis in Health Research
With Examples From Tobacco Control

Level of Analysis	Example From Research Programs in Tobacco Control
Cultural/political	Measuring elasticity of the effect of cigarette taxation on population smoking rates
Social/environmental	Measuring the relative importance of family and peer environment on teen smoking incidence
Behavioral/psychological	Designing effective smoking prevention and cessation programs
Organ systems	Designing ways to block tumor formation in smokers
Cellular	Tracing metabolic pathways of nicotine uptake
Molecular/genetic	Examining the genetic basis of nicotine dependence

Institute of Medicine report on the future of public health. Figure 1.1, based on Figure S-1 from Gebbie, Rosenstock, and Hernandez (2003), shows an ecological model of the determinants of health. The IOM report emphasizes that public health professionals, including health researchers, must understand and utilize just such an ecological approach if they are to be successful at improving the nation's health in the future.

Theoretical Reasons for Multilevel Models

The simplest argument, then, for multilevel modeling techniques is this: Because so much of what we study is multilevel in nature, we should use theories and analytic techniques that are also multilevel. If we do not do this, we can run into serious problems.

For example, it is very common to collect and analyze health and behavioral data at the aggregate level. Epidemiologic studies, for example, have shown that in countries where fat is a larger component of the diet, the death rate from breast cancer is also higher (Carroll, 1975). It might seem

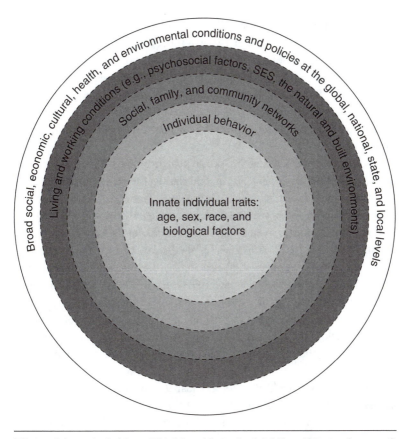

Figure 1.1   A Guide to Thinking About the Multilevel Determinants of
Health

Source: Adapted from Gebbie, Rosenstock, and Hernandez (2003).

reasonable to then assume that women who eat a lot of fat would be more
likely to get breast cancer. However, this interpretation is an example of the
ecological fallacy, where relationships observed in groups are assumed to
hold for individuals (Freedman, 1999). Recent health studies, in fact, have
suggested that the link between fat intake and breast cancer is not very strong
at the individual level (Holmes et al., 1999).

    This type of problem can also work the other way. It is very common in
the behavioral sciences to collect data from individuals and then aggregate
the data to gain insight into the groups to which those individuals belong.

This can lead to the *atomistic fallacy,* where inferences about groups are incorrectly drawn from individual-level information (Hox, 2002). It is possible to be successful assessing ecological characteristics from individual-level data; for example, see Moos's work on social climates (Moos, 1996). However, as Shinn and Rapkin (2000) have convincingly argued, this approach is fraught with danger, and a much more valid approach is to assess group and ecological characteristics using group-level measures and analytic tools.

It is useful here to consider the sociological distinction between properties of *collectives* and *members* (Lazarsfeld and & Menzel, 1969). Members belong to collectives, but various properties (variables) of both collectives and their members may be measured and analyzed at the same time. Lazarsfeld and Menzel identify analytical, structural, and global properties of collectives. *Analytical* properties are obtained by aggregating information from the individual members of the collective (e.g., proportion of Hispanics in a city). *Structural* properties are based on the relational characteristics of collective members (e.g., friendship density in a classroom). Finally, *global* properties are characteristics of the collective itself that are not based on the properties of the individual members (O'Brien, 2000). Presence of an anti-smoking policy in a school would be a global property of the school, for example.

Using this framework, it becomes clear that fallacies are a problem of *inference,* not of *measurement.* That is, it is perfectly admissible to characterize a higher-level collective using information obtained from lower-level members. The types of fallacies described above come about when relationships discovered at one particular level are inappropriately assumed to occur in the same fashion at some other (higher or lower) level.

Statistical Reasons for Multilevel Models

When confronted with these very difficult conceptual problems, social scientists have tended to utilize traditional individual-level statistical tools for their data, even if their data and hypotheses are multilevel in nature. One approach has been to disaggregate group-level information to the individual level so that all predictors in a multiple regression model are tied to the individual unit of analysis. This leads to at least two problems. First, all of the un-modeled contextual information ends up pooled into the single individual error term of the model (Duncan, Jones, & Moon, 1998). This is problematic because individuals belonging to the same context will presumably have correlated errors, which violates one of the basic assumptions of multiple regression. The second problem is that by ignoring context, the model assumes that the regression coefficients apply equally to all contexts, "thus propagating the notion that processes work out in the same way in different contexts" (Duncan et al., 1998, p. 98).

One partial solution to these statistical problems is to include an effect in the model that corresponds to the grouping of the individuals. This leads to an ANOVA or ANCOVA approach to modeling. Unfortunately, there are still a number of issues with this approach. First, in the case where there are many groups, these models will have many more parameters, resulting in greatly reduced power and parsimony. Second, these group parameters are often treated as fixed effects, which ignores the random variability associated with group-level characteristics. Finally, ANOVA methods are not very flexible in handling missing data or greatly unbalanced designs.

Scope of Book

Based on the previous discussion, the purpose of this monograph is to provide a relatively non-technical introduction to multilevel modeling statistical techniques for social and health scientists. After this introduction, the book is split into two major sections. Chapter 2 introduces the two-level multilevel model and describes the steps in fitting a multilevel model, including data preparation, model estimation, model interpretation, hypothesis testing, testing of model assumptions, and centering. Chapter 3 covers useful extensions to the basic multilevel model including modeling non-continuous and non-normal dependent variables, using multilevel models with longitudinal data, and building three-level models. The presentation of these topics only assumes familiarity with multiple regression, and the text makes extensive use of example data and analyses. (All of the data, programs, and output are available from the author–see Appendix.) All of the statistical analyses were performed using HLM Version 5.04 (Raudenbush, Bryk, Cheong, & Congdon, 2000) and the *nlme* Version 3.1 mixed-effects library in R (Pinheiro, Bates, DebRoy, & Sarkar, 2003); all graphics were produced using R Version 1.7.1.

A useful definition to serve as a basis for the rest of the presentation is as follows: A multilevel model is a statistical model applied to data

8

TABLE 1.2
Types of Multilevel Models and Structures
Found in the Health and Social Sciences

Type of Multilevel Model	Multilevel Structure	Examples
Physical	Entities nested within the immediate physical environment, including the biological, ecological, and physically built environments	Diez-Roux et al. (2001) Perkins et al. (1993)
Social	Entities nested within social structures, including families, peer groups, and other types of social networks	Buka et al. (2003) Rice et al. (1998)
Organizational	Individuals and small groups nested within specific organizational contexts. Important organizational characteristics include size, management structure, communication aspects, organizational goals, and so on	Maes and Lievens (2003) Villemez and Bridges (1988)
Political/cultural	Individuals or groups of individuals nested within specific sociopolitical, cultural, or historical contexts	Lochner et al. (2001) Luke and Krauss (2004)
Temporal	Multiple observations of a single entity taken over time	Boyle and Willms (2001) Curran, Stice, and Chassin (1997)
Analytic	Multiple-effect measures nested within individual studies (i.e., meta-analysis)	Goldstein et al. (2000) Raudenbush and Bryk (1985)

collected at more than one level in order to elucidate relationships at more than one level. The statistical basis for multilevel modeling has been developed over the past several decades from a number of different disciplines, and has been called various things, including hierarchical linear models

(Raudenbush & Bryk, 2002), random coefficient models (Longford, 1993), mixed-effects models (Pinheiro & Bates, 2000), covariance structure models (Muthén, 1994) growth-curve models (McArdle & Epstein, 1987), as well as multilevel models. All of these specific types of multilevel models fall into one of two broad statistical categories: a multiple regression approach and a structural equation modeling approach. This book will focus on the multiple regression-based multilevel modeling. For a good introduction to the SEM-based approach, see Chapters 5–7 in Heck and Thomas (2000).

Multilevel models are starting to appear more frequently in every area of the social and health sciences, as the techniques have become more widely known and integrated into the major statistical packages. There are as many specific types of multilevel models as there are scientific questions. However, there are certain types of overarching models that can be seen across the different research disciplines, as indicated in Table 1.2. This table is not meant to be exhaustive, but to provide a catalyst for the reader and indicate the extremely wide applicability of multilevel methods. In particular, it is not immediately obvious to the new analyst that multilevel techniques can be extremely useful for modeling longitudinal data (where multiple observations are nested within an individual) and also for meta-analytic studies (where multiple effect statistics are nested within individual studies).

2. BASIC MULTILEVEL MODELING

The Basic Two-Level Multilevel Model

The goal of a multilevel model is to predict values of some dependent variable based on a function of predictor variables at more than one level. For example, we might want to examine how a child's score on a standardized reading exam is influenced both by characteristics of the child (e.g., amount of study time) as well as characteristics of the child's classroom (e.g., size of class). In this example, we consider the child to be measured and modeled at level-1, and the classroom at level-2.

This simple two-level structure can be seen in the following multilevel model, with one predictor variable each at level-1 and level-2:

Equation 2.1

$$\text{Level 1:} \quad Y_{ij} = \beta_{0j} + \beta_{1j} X_{ij} + r_{ij}$$
$$\text{Level 2:} \quad \beta_{0j} = \gamma_{00} + \gamma_{01} W_j + u_{0j}$$
$$\beta_{1j} = \gamma_{10} + \gamma_{11} W_j + u_{1j}$$

This system of equations not only lists all of the predictor and dependent variables, but also clearly delineates the multilevel nature of the model. The level-1 part of the model looks similar to a typical OLS multiple regression model. However, the j subscripts tell us that a different level-1 model is being estimated for each of the j level-2 units (classrooms). Using the above example, each classroom in the study may have a different average reading score (β_{0j}) and a different effect of study time on reading score (β_{1j}). Thus, we are allowing the intercept and slope to vary across the level-2 units. This leads to the critical conception in multilevel modeling—we can treat intercepts and slopes as outcomes of level-2 predictors.

The level-2 part of the model listed in Equation 2.1 indicates how each of the level-1 parameters are functions of level-2 predictors and variability: β_{0j} is the level-1 intercept in level-2 unit j; γ_{00} is the mean value of the level-1 dependent variable, controlling for the level-2 predictor, W_j; γ_{01} is the effect (slope) of the level-2 predictor, W_j; and u_{0j} is the error, or unmodeled variability, for unit j. The interpretation of the second equation is similar, but here we are modeling the level-2 effects on the slope of X_{ij}: β_{1j} is the level-1 slope in level-2 unit j; γ_{10} is the mean value of the level-1 slope, controlling for the level-2 predictor, W_j; γ_{11} is the effect of the level-2 predictor, W_j; and u_{1j} is the error for unit j.

Instead of using a *system of equations* to specify the multilevel model, we can substitute the level-2 parts of the model into the level-1 equation. After substituting and rearranging the terms, we get the following:

Equation 2.2

$$Y_{ij} = [\gamma_{00} + \gamma_{10} X_{ij} + \gamma_{01} W_j + \gamma_{11} W_j X_{ij}] + [u_{0j} + u_{1j} X_{ij} + r_{ij}].$$
$$\qquad\qquad\qquad\quad \textit{fixed} \qquad\qquad\qquad\qquad\qquad \textit{random}$$

This single prediction equation form of the multilevel model is sometimes called the *mixed-effects model*—it is more compact, but it is harder to quickly discern the multilevel structure of the underlying model. However, this form has two advantages. First, as shown above, the single prediction equation clearly indicates which part of the model is composed of fixed effects (the γs) and which part is composed of random effects (u and r). This illustrates why multilevel models are also called mixed models or mixed-effects models; they are always made up of both fixed and random effects. The other advantage of the single prediction equation form is that it closely corresponds to the output of multilevel modeling software. In addition, this form makes it clear that the level-1 parameters (i.e., β_{0j}, β_{1j}) are not directly estimated, but are indirectly estimated through the level-2 gammas (γ).

Most analysts, especially those who utilize ANOVA methods, are familiar with fixed effects. Random effects, on the other hand, may be a little less familiar. In the context of ANOVA, random effects are often defined as independent factors whose levels have been randomly selected from a larger potential population of factor levels. In multilevel modeling, however, it is more useful to think of random effects as additional error terms or sources of variability. In our classroom example, we have the traditional individual-level error term: r_{ij}. However, our multilevel model has two additional error terms: u_{0j} is the variability of reading scores between classrooms, and u_{1j} is the variability of the relationship of study time to reading scores between classrooms. So, a multilevel model will generally have random effects that are tied to level-1 and level-2 units.

Equation 2.1 illustrates a fairly typical multilevel model, but there are many types of multilevel models that may be estimated depending on the situation. To get a handle on the bewildering array of possible models, it helps to see that the final form of the model will depend on the following decisions:

1. How many levels are in your data, and how many of these levels do you want to model? Although it is possible to include more than 3 levels in a model, most published examples in the social science literature are of 2 or 3 levels.
2. How many predictors at each level do you want to consider?
3. Do you want to model level-1 intercepts, slopes, or intercepts *and* slopes as a function of level-2 characteristics? Figure 2.1 shows the difference between (a) intercepts-as-outcomes, and (b) slopes *and* intercepts-as-outcomes. The left side of the figure shows a model that has constant slope across the level-2 units, but varying intercepts. The right side shows both intercepts and slopes as varying. The analyst

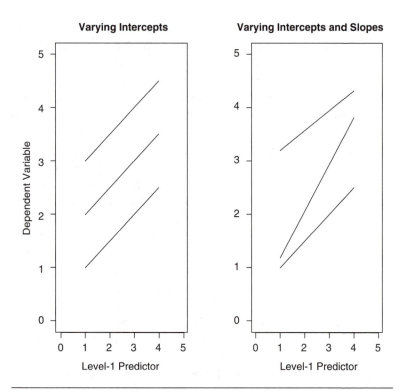

Figure 2.1 Example of Intercepts-as-Outcomes and Intercepts and Slopes-as-Outcomes for Three Level-2 Units

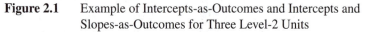

should use both theory and evidence from the data to help guide this decision.

4. Finally, which parts of the model should include random effects?

Despite the large number of different multilevel models that a researcher may wish to use, it is helpful to think about three broad classes of multilevel models, listed in Table 2.1. The first type of model is the simplest possible multilevel model that has no level-1 or level-2 predictors. This unconstrained, or null-model, is often used as a starting point for building more complex models. It is particularly useful for calculating the intraclass correlation coefficient (ICC) (see below).

The second class of models assumes that level-1 intercepts vary across level-2 units, but not the level-1 slopes. We would use this class of model in

TABLE 2.1
Three Classes of Multilevel Models

Class	System of Equations Model	Mixed-Effects Model	Description	Notes
1. Unconstrained	L1: $Y_{ij} = \beta_{0j} + r_{ij}$ L2: $\beta_{0j} = \gamma_{00} + u_{0j}$	$Y_{ij} = \gamma_{00} + u_{0j} + r_{ij}$	One-way random effects ANOVA	Often used as a null model to estimate between-groups effects with an ICC
2. Random intercepts	L1: $Y_{ij} = \beta_{0j} + r_{ij}$ L2: $\beta_{0j} = \gamma_{00} + \gamma_{01} W_j + u_{0j}$	$Y_{ij} = \gamma_{00} + \gamma_{01} W_j + u_{0j} + r_{ij}$	Means as outcomes	Here the emphasis is on L2 predictors.
	L1: $Y_{ij} = \beta_{0j} + \beta_{1j} X_{ij} + r_{ij}$ L2: $\beta_{0j} = \gamma_{00} + u_{0j}$ $\beta_{1j} = \gamma_{10}$	$Y_{ij} = \gamma_{00} + \gamma_{10} X_{ij} + u_{0j} + r_{ij}$	One-way random effects ANCOVA	

(Continued)

13

TABLE 2.1
(Continued)

Class	System of Equations Model	Mixed-Effects Model	Description	Notes
3. Random intercepts and slopes	L1: $Y_{ij} = \beta_{0j} + \beta_{1j} X_j + r_{ij}$ L2: $\beta_{0j} = \gamma_{00} + u_{0j}$ $\beta_{1j} = \gamma_{10} + u_{1j}$	$Y_{ij} = \gamma_{00} + \gamma_{10} X_{ij} + u_{0j}$ $+ u_{ij} X_{ij} + r_{ij}$	Random coefficients regression model	Intercepts and slopes of L1 model are allowed to vary across L2 units, but we are not modeling that variability with L2 predictors
	L1: $Y_{ij} = \beta_{0j} + \beta_{1j} X_j + r_{ij}$ L2: $\beta_{0j} = \gamma_{00} + \gamma_{01} W_j + u_{0j}$ $\beta_{1j} = \gamma_{10} + \gamma_{11} W_j + u_{1j}$	$Y_{ij} = \gamma_{00} + \gamma_{01} W_j + \gamma_{10} X_{ij}$ $+ \gamma_{11} W_j X_{ij}$ $+ u_{1j} X_{ij} + r_{ij}$	Intercepts and slopes as outcomes	Level-1 intercept and slopes are modeled using Level-2 predictor(s). Note the cross-level interaction component: $(\gamma_{11} W_j X_{ij})$

our example if we believed that different classrooms had different average reading scores, but believed that the effects of individual study time on reading ability were the same across classrooms. The final class of models assumes that both intercepts *and* slopes vary across level-2 units. We would use this model if we believed that there was a cross-level interaction between classroom characteristics and individual study time on reading scores. For example, some teachers may get better results only with students who study a great deal, whereas other teachers may have a positive effect on all students regardless of study time. Note that this type of cross-level interaction effect is made explicit by the $\gamma_{11} W_j X_{ij}$ term in the single prediction equation form of the multilevel model (Equation 2.2).

How to Build and Evaluate a Multilevel Model

Introduction to Tobacco Industry Data Set

To illustrate how to develop, test, and interpret a typical multilevel model, I will use an example data set taken from a tobacco control policy study (all data used here are available for download—see Appendix). The main goal of this study was to identify the important influences on voting on tobacco-related legislation by members of Congress from 1997 to 2000 (Luke & Krauss, 2004). The dependent variable is *Voting %*, the percentage of time that a senator or representative voted in a "pro-tobacco" direction during those four years. As an example, consider the 1998 Senate Bill S1415–144, which was an amendment proposed by Senator Ted Kennedy (D-Mass.) to raise federal cigarette taxes by $1.50 per pack over three years. For our purposes, a "No" vote is considered to be a "pro-tobacco" vote because the tobacco industry opposed this legislation. This particular bill was defeated, 40–58. *Voting %* was calculated for each member of Congress by adding up the total number of times that he or she voted in a pro-industry direction, and dividing by the total number of tobacco-related bills that he or she voted on. The variable can range from 0.0 (never voted pro-tobacco) to 1.0 (always voted pro-tobacco). (There are problems in modeling a dependent variable that is a percentage or proportion. This is discussed in Chapter 3.)

Party records the political party of each legislator. Past research has shown that political party is an important predictor of voting pattern—Republicans tend to vote more often in the pro-tobacco industry direction. The other

16

TABLE 2.2
Structure of Level-1 Tobacco Data Set

Name	Branch	State	VotePct	Party	Money ($K)
Murkowski	Senate	AK	.84	Republican	9.2
Young	House	AK	.57	Republican	23.5
Shelby	Senate	AL	.64	Republican	24.2
Cramer	House	AL	.89	Democrat	14.0
...					

NOTE: $N = 527$.

important individual-level variable in which we are interested is *Money,* the amount of money that the member of Congress received from tobacco industry political action committees (PACs). Our hypothesis is that the more PAC money a legislator receives, the more often that person will vote pro-tobacco.

In addition to these level-1 variables, we will also have information about the level-2 units. First of all, we will need to know which state each member of Congress represents. Then, we will need to obtain any level-2 variables that we want to use in our model. The most important level-2 factor in our model is the state tobacco farm economy. We measure this with *Acres,* the number of harvested acres of tobacco in 1999, in thousands of acres.

Although many multilevel software packages allow you to combine the level-1 and level-2 information into a single data file (e.g., SAS and S-Plus), HLM has you start out with two data files, one for each of the levels in your model. Tables 2.2 and 2.3 show how the data sets for our tobacco study are structured. An important element of the level-1 data file is the linking or index variable that connects each level-1 case to the appropriate level-2 unit. The state abbreviation serves as the link variable for this data set. HLM requires that the data set be sorted on the link variable. Note that the minimal data requirement for a multilevel analysis is a dependent variable and a link to a level-2 unit. However, in most cases, the data sets will also include a variety of level-1 and level-2 predictor variables.

For software that requires only one data file, the file will be organized at the lowest level of analysis. Any level-2 (or higher) predictors will be disaggregated and included in each level-1 record. So, for example, to analyze the tobacco data set in *nlme* in S-Plus, one data set is prepared

TABLE 2.3
Structure of Level-2 Tobacco Data Set

State	Acres
AK	0.0
AL	0.0
AR	0.0
...	

NOTE: $N = 50$.

with 527 records, one for each member of Congress. In addition to the index variable (*State*) and the level-1 predictors, each case will also have a value for *Acres*. This is a disaggregated level-2 predictor; every member of Congress from the same state will have the same value for this variable.

Assessing the Need for a Multilevel Model

The first step in building a multilevel model is to decide whether a multilevel model is even needed in the first place. In general, we can use three types of justification for a multilevel model: empirical, statistical, and theoretical. Following along with our tobacco policy example, each of these three justifications will be discussed in turn.

Figure 2.2 displays the average pro-tobacco voting percentage for members of Congress for each state. This map shows that there is considerable variability from state to state on voting behavior. In particular, the southeastern and Plains states appear to vote most often for tobacco industry interests, whereas New England tends to vote against the industry. Further evidence of state variability is shown in Figure 2.3, a scatter plot of the relationship between PAC contributions received and voting behavior for five of the largest states. For all five of the states, there appears to be a positive relationship between PAC contributions and pro-tobacco voting percentage. New York has the lowest pro-tobacco average score of the group. Also, two of the states (CA and IL) appear to have a much stronger relationship (steeper slope) between money and voting than the other states. A much more detailed graphical examination is provided in Figure 2.4, which is a trellis plot of the within-state linear fits that can be obtained in S-Plus or R (Becker & Cleveland, 1996). (As we shall see later when we

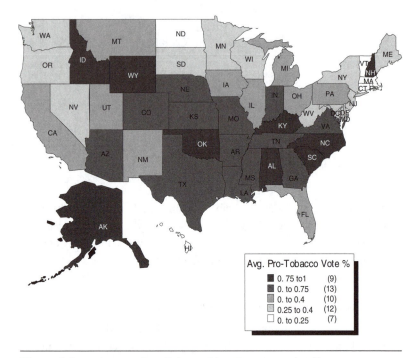

Figure 2.2   Average Pro-Tobacco Vote Percentage by Congress
Members–1997 to 2000

discuss diagnostics, S-Plus/R provides a much richer and more flexible set of graphical tools than any other major statistics package.) This graph also shows that voting percentage increases with PAC money. However, we can see very clearly here the extent of the state-to-state variability. For example, even though most states show a positive relationship between PAC money and pro-tobacco voting, some states, such as Oklahoma and Michigan, do not. Also, we can see that some states (the small states with few representatives) are contributing relatively less information than other larger states.

Graphical techniques such as these can be extremely useful for gathering empirical evidence of the need for multilevel modeling. A more formal piece of empirical evidence is provided by the intraclass correlation coefficient (ICC). The ICC measures the proportion of variance in the dependent variable that is accounted for by groups (i.e., level-2 units):

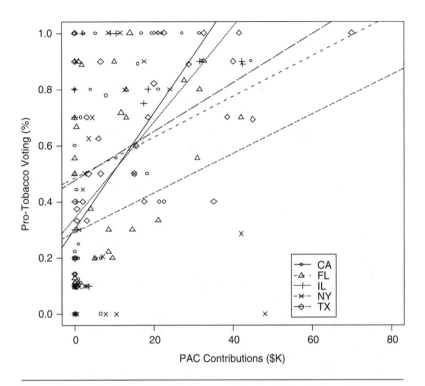

Figure 2.3   Relationship of Money and Voting % for 5 Large States

Equation 2.3

$$\rho = \frac{\sigma_{u_0}^2}{(\sigma_{u_0}^2 + \sigma_r^2)},$$

where $\sigma_{u_0}^2$ and σ_r^2 are estimates of the level-2 and level-1 variances, respectively, and are obtained by fitting a null-model using multilevel modeling software such as HLM or *Proc MIXED* in SAS, or *nlme* in S-Plus or R.

Tables 2.4 and 2.5 show partial output for the null, unconstrained model using HLM and R, respectively. Remember that the null model is a multilevel model with no level-1 or level-2 predictors:

Equation 2.4

Level 1: $Y_{ij} = \beta_{0j} + r_{ij}$

Level 2: $\beta_{0j} = \gamma_{00} + u_{0j}$

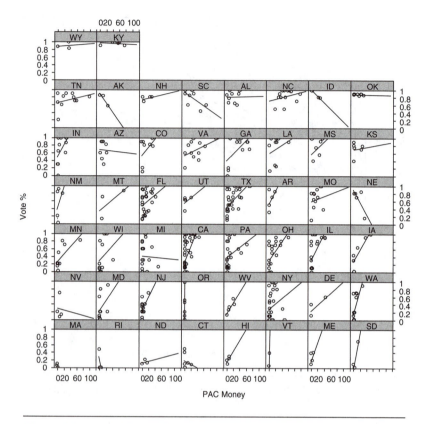

Figure 2.4   OLS Fits of Voting % and Money for 50 States

The mixed-effects form of this model is then:

Equation 2.5

$$Y_{ij} = \gamma_{00} + u_{0j} + r_{ij}.$$

Y_{ij} is the voting percentage for a particular legislator within a particular state. The only fixed effect (γ_{00}) is the grand mean across all members of Congress. The error is split into two components—the variability between states (u_{0j}) and the variability between legislators within a state (r_{ij}). We can see that this null model is the same as a one-way, random-effects ANOVA model.

For both HLM and R, the estimate for the level-2 variance is .035 and for level-1 is .093. (R reports the random effects in standard deviation

TABLE 2.4

Partial *HLM* Output for the Null Model

Random level-1	coefficient	Reliability estimate
INTRCPT1, B0		0.729

The value of the likelihood function at iteration $7 = -1.559344E + 002$
The outcome variable is VOTEPCT
Final estimation of fixed effects:

Fixed Effect	Coefficient	Standard Error	T-ratio	Approx. d.f.	P-value
For INTRCPT1, B0					
INTRCPT2, G00	0.530942	0.031142	17.049	49	0.000

Final estimation of variance components:

Random Effect		Standard Deviation	Variance Component	df	Chi-square	P-value
INTRCPT1,	U0	0.18798	0.03534	49	214.13316	0.000
level-1,	R	0.30436	0.09264			

Statistics for current covariance components model

Deviance = 311.868804
Number of estimated parameters = 3

units, whereas HLM gives the random effects in both standard deviation and variance units.) The ICC is then $.035/(.093 + .035) = .27$. This means that states account for 27% of the variability of voting behavior among legislators. This moderately high ICC value suggests that a multilevel model incorporating states and state characteristics may be useful.

Note that because there are no level-1 or 2 predictor variables in the null-model, there is only one fixed effect estimated. The estimate for γ_{00} is .53, which is interpreted as the average value of the dependent variable across all subjects. Thus, a typical senator or representative is expected to vote pro-tobacco slightly more than half of the time.

The second justification for using a multilevel model arises from the statistical or structural properties of the data. A major assumption of single-level, ordinary least squares (OLS) models is that the observations (and hence the error terms) are independent from one another. Whenever there is

TABLE 2.5

Partial *R* Output for the Null Model

Linear mixed-effects model fit by maximum likelihood
  Data: RSGrp

	AIC	BIC	loglik
	319.7067	332.5083	−156.8533

Random effects:
  Formula: ~1 | state

	(Intercept)	Residual
StdDev:	0.1879767	0.3043614

Fixed effects: votepct ~ 1

	Value	Std.Error	DF	t-value	p-value
(Intercept)	0.530942	0.03116992	477	17.03379	< .0001

Standardized Within-Group Residuals:

Min	Q1	Med	Q3	Max
−2.23742030	−0.85314980	0.03887117	0.75954570	2.10386071

Number of Observations: 527
Number of Groups: 50

---

a nested structure in a data set, there is a good chance that the independence assumption is violated. The moderately large ICC in our example already suggests that our observations are not independent. This makes sense given the clustered nature of our data. Senators and representatives from North Carolina, for example, are probably more similar to each other than they are to Congress members from other states, such as Massachusetts. As the saying goes, all politics are local, and it is reasonable to assume that state characteristics can shape political behavior as much as other individual factors, such as political party.

Multilevel modeling relaxes this independence assumption, and allows for correlated error structures. If OLS is used inappropriately for clustered data with correlated errors, the resulting standard errors are smaller than they should be, resulting in a greater chance of committing Type I errors. Multilevel models, on the other hand, will estimate the appropriate, unbiased, errors.

The final, and most important justification for using multilevel models is theoretical. Any time a researcher utilizes a theoretical framework or poses hypotheses that are composed of constructs operating and interacting at multiple levels, then the researcher should use multilevel statistical models. This may seem obvious, but as discussed in Chapter 1, it is quite common to see published work where the theoretical approach is multilevel, but the data are collected and/or the analyses are performed at a single level. For our tobacco voting study, it is reasonable to hypothesize that characteristics of the state of a legislator may influence his or her voting on tobacco-related bills. Specifically, one hypothesis that we will test is that legislators from states with strong tobacco farming economies will be more likely to vote pro-tobacco than legislators from states with no tobacco economy.

So, using our example, we have seen the three types of justification for building a multilevel model. The empirical justification comes from examining the data using graphical tools, and seeing that voting (level-1) varies strongly by state (level-2). This is also confirmed with the substantial ICC. The statistical justification comes from recognizing that the cases in our study are not independent, are clustered by state, and are likely to exhibit correlated errors. Finally, the theoretical justification comes from our interest in a multilevel model that will examine how state-level characteristics influence individual voting behavior.

Moving From Simple to More Complex Models

There is no single best way to build a multilevel model—the individual steps that a researcher should take in building the model are based on the investigator's research questions; whether the analysis is exploratory or confirmatory; and whether the analytic emphasis is on parameter estimation, model fit, or prediction (Harrell, 2001). All other things being equal, however, a typical approach is to build the model from the bottom up. First, start with the level-1 predictors. Once the level-1 model is satisfactory, examine potential level-2 predictors. Initially, consider an intercept-as-outcome model for the level-2 predictors. Finally, if there is empirical evidence and theoretical justification, examine a slopes-as-outcomes model. All three of these stages will now be illustrated with our tobacco data set. As the full model is being built, other important statistical issues will be discussed, including estimation techniques, hypothesis testing, effect sizes, model diagnostics, and prediction.

Our first step is to build a simple model with only level-1 predictors that we will call Model 1.

Equation 2.6

$$\text{VotePct} = \beta_{0j} + \beta_{1j}(\text{Party})_{ij} + \beta_{2j}(\text{Money})_{ij} + r_{ij}$$
$$\beta_{0j} = \gamma_{00} + u_{0j}$$
$$\beta_{1j} = \gamma_{10} + u_{1j}$$
$$\beta_{2j} = \gamma_{20} + u_{2j}$$

The two level-1 predictors are *Party* (0 = Democrat; 1 = Republican) and *Money* (PAC money received, in thousands of dollars). There are no level-2 predictors, although we are allowing the level-1 intercept and slopes to vary across states. Therefore, Model 1 has three fixed effects, and four random effects (i.e., one intercept, two slopes, and the level-1 error). This can be seen more clearly with the mixed-effects form of the model:

Equation 2.7

$$\text{VotePct} = \gamma_{00} + \gamma_{10}(\text{Party})_{ij} + \gamma_{20}(\text{Money})_{ij}$$
$$+ u_{0j} + u_{1j}(\text{Party})_{ij} + u_{2j}(\text{Money})_{ij} + r_{ij}.$$

Tables 2.6 and 2.7 show partial HLM and R output for Model 1. The beginning of the HLM output lists summary information that is useful to recreate the analyses. It is particularly important to examine the summary of the model to ensure that the program is estimating the correct model.

The essential components of the fitted multilevel model are the statistical parameters: the fixed effects regression parameters (the gammas) and the variance components for the random effects. It is important to keep in mind that the level-2 errors (U0, U1, and U2 in the output) are not statistical parameters, per se, but are latent random variables, with an expected mean of 0, and variance = σ_u^2.

The estimate for γ_{00} is .22. This is no longer interpreted as the grand mean of voting percentage; instead, it is the expected value of voting percentage when the predictor values are all 0. So, according to these data, Democratic legislators who have received no money from tobacco industry PACs are expected to vote pro-tobacco only 22% of the time. The estimate of γ_{10} is .48, which tells us that the "effect" of being Republican is to vote pro-tobacco 48% more often compared to Democrats. Finally, $\gamma_{20} = .0046$, which tells us that for every \$1,000 received by a legislator, we would expect to see an increase in pro-tobacco voting of approximately 0.46%.

TABLE 2.6
Partial *HLM* Output for Model 1

Problem Title: ANALYSIS 2–2A – LEVEL-1 MODEL; ML

The data source for this run = Sage1.ssm
The command file for this run = whlmtemp.hlm
Output file name = G:\HLM\analyses\an12–2a.out
The maximum number of level-2 units = 50
The maximum number of iterations = 2000
Method of estimation: full maximum likelihood

The outcome variable is VOTEPCT

The model specified for the fixed effects was:

Level-1 Coefficients		Level-2 Predictors	
INTRCPT1,	B0	INTRCPT2,	G00
PARTY slope,	B1	INTRCPT2,	G10
MONEY slope,	B2	INTRCPT2,	G20

Summary of the model specified (in equation format)

Level-1 Model
$$Y = B0 + B1*(PARTY) + B2*(MONEY) + R$$
Level-2 Model
$$B0 = G00 + U0$$
$$B1 = G10 + U1$$
$$B2 = G20 + U2$$

The outcome variable is VOTEPCT

Final estimation of fixed effects (with robust standard errors)

Fixed Effect	Coefficient	Standard Error	T-ratio	Approx. d.f.	P-value
For INTRCPT1, B0					
INTRCPT2, G00	0.219654	0.024514	8.960	49	0.000
For PARTY slope, B1					
INTRCPT2, G10	0.480382	0.021969	21.866	49	0.000
For MONEY slope, B2					
INTRCPT2, G20	0.004650	0.000416	11.185	49	0.000

(Continued)

TABLE 2.6

(Continued)

Final estimation of variance components:

Random Effect		Standard Deviation	Variance Component	df	Chi-square	P-value
INTRCPT1,	U0	0.13660	0.01866	37	122.02858	0.000
PARTY slope,	U1	0.08967	0.00804	37	67.04921	0.002
MONEY slope,	U2	0.00125	0.00000	37	36.84181	> .500
level-1,	R	0.16379	0.02683			

Statistics for current covariance components model

Deviance $= -332.009660$
Number of estimated parameters $= 10$

The random effects part of the model is concerned with the variance components. These should not be interpreted as "effects" in the model. Instead, non-zero variance components are evidence of un-modeled variability. This information can be used to help decide either to add more variables to the model, or, conversely, to stop adding variables at a particular level. The relatively large variance components for level-1 (.027) and level-2 (.019) can thus be interpreted as evidence that we might want to consider adding more predictors to the model.

Estimation

It is most common to use some type of maximum likelihood estimation when fitting basic multilevel models. As noted in the above output, our level-1 model was fit using maximum likelihood (ML). Another closely related method that can be used is restricted maximum likelihood (REML). What are the differences between these two methods, and how can you choose which method to use? The main practical difference between the two is how the random-effects variance components are calculated. Both methods, in fact, produce exactly the same fixed-effects estimates. REML takes into account the degrees of freedom of the fixed effects when estimating the variance components. This results in random-effects estimates that are less biased than with full ML. However, these differences are usually quite

TABLE 2.7
Partial *R* Output for Model 1

Linear mixed-effects model fit by maximum likelihood
Data: RSGrp
                AIC   BIC   logLik
                −308.5973   −265.9253   164.2987

Random effects:
  Formula: ~money + party | state
  Structure: General positive-definite, Log-Cholesky parameterization
                    StdDev   Corr
(Intercept)   0.134575268   (Intr)   money
money   0.001357522   −0.713
partyRepublican 0.086057425   −0.814   0.436
Residual   0.163656400

Fixed effects: votepct ~ money + party
                    Value   Std.Error   DF   t-value   p-value
(Intercept)   0.2184723   0.024406748   475   8.951306   <.0001
money   0.0045613   0.000511181   475   8.923085   <.0001
partyRepublican 0.4824129   0.021664475   475   22.267461   <.0001
  Correlation:
                    (Intr)   money
money   −0.402
partyRepublican −0.703   −0.029

Standardized Within-Group Residuals:
        Min   Q1   Med   Q3   Max
    −3.62445062   −0.59380990   −0.01877607   0.54601215   4.46844056

Number of Observations: 527
Number of Groups: 50

small, especially when there is a relatively large number of level-2 units, on the order of 30 or more (Snijders & Bosker, 1999). Another important advantage of ML is that the deviance statistic produced by full ML can be used to compare the fixed and random effects of two models (see the section on Assessing Model Fit that follows).

Table 2.8 shows the random-effects part of the level-1 model using both ML and REML. As can be seen, in our data set with 50 level-2 units, the

TABLE 2.8

Comparison of Random Effects Estimates for ML and REML

Random Effect	Full Maximum Likelihood (ML)			Restricted Maximum Likelihood (REML)		
	Variance Component	Chi-Square	p Value	Variance Component	Chi-Square	p Value
Intercept	.01866	122.03	.000	.01942	122.05	.000
Party slope	.00804	67.05	.002	.00860	66.96	.002
Money slope	.00000	36.84	> .500	.00000	36.73	> .500
Level-1	.02683			.02686		

differences between the two methods are trivial, and would not lead to any important difference in model-building or interpretation. For most purposes, then, use full ML unless you have a small number of level-2 units and the two methods produce large differences.

The random-effects variance components in our model are all greater than zero, suggesting that there is potentially substantial un-modeled variability. This leads to our next two models (Models 2 and 3), where we add a level-2 predictor, the number of acres of tobacco harvested in a state. First, we will have Acres influence only the intercept (β_{0j}) of the level-1 prediction equation:

Equation 2.8

$$\text{VotePct} = \beta_{0j} + \beta_{1j}(\text{Party})_{ij} + \beta_{2j}(\text{Money})_{ij} + r_{ij}$$
$$\beta_{0j} = \gamma_{00} + \gamma_{01}(\text{Acres})_j + u_{0j}$$
$$\beta_{1j} = \gamma_{10} + u_{1j}$$
$$\beta_{2j} = \gamma_{20} + u_{2j}$$

The intent of this "intercept" model is to assess the extent to which the interstate variability of voting behavior can be explained by a simple measure of the extensiveness of the tobacco economy within a state.

The next logical extension of this model is to allow tobacco acreage to influence the slopes of the two level-1 predictors, Party and Money:

Equation 2.9

$$\text{VotePct} = \beta_{0j} + \beta_{1j}(\text{Party})_{ij} + \beta_{2j}(\text{Money})_{ij} + r_{ij}$$
$$\beta_{0j} = \gamma_{00} + \gamma_{01}(\text{Acres})_j + u_{0j}$$
$$\beta_{1j} = \gamma_{10} + \gamma_{11}(\text{Acres})_j + u_{1j}$$
$$\beta_{2j} = \gamma_{20} + \gamma_{21}(\text{Acres})_j + u_{2j}$$

This "slopes" model (Model 3) will test not only whether tobacco acreage influences average voting behavior in a state, but also whether it interacts with either of the two level-1 predictors. Thus, the parameters γ_{11} and γ_{21} are serving as indications of cross-level interactions where a level-2 characteristic may influence a level-1 relationship. The mixed-effects form of the model is as follows:

Equation 2.10

$$\text{VotePct} = \gamma_{00} + \gamma_{01}(A)_j + \gamma_{10}(P)_{ij} + \gamma_{11}(A)_j(P)_{ij}$$
$$+ \gamma_{20}(M)_{ij} + \gamma_{21}(A)_j(M)_{ij}$$
$$+ u_{0j} + u_{1j}(P)_{ij} + u_{2j}(M)_{ij} + r_{ij}$$

where A is Acres, P is Party, and M is Money.

Testing the Model: Hypothesis Testing

Table 2.9 presents the important results from each of these last three models. In order to understand these results, we need to understand how hypothesis testing of individual parameter estimates and model comparisons are handled in multilevel models. Significance tests for fixed-effects parameters (the gammas) are similar to those for multiple regression. In the HLM software, the estimated parameter coefficient divided by its standard error forms a t-ratio with degrees of freedom of $J - p - 1$, where J is the number of level-2 units and p is the number of level-2 predictors. Most other multilevel software programs use the typical ML Wald Test to test for

TABLE 2.9
Parameter Estimates and Model Fit for Three Models

Fixed Effects	Model 1				Model 2				Model 3			
	Coef.	SE	T-ratio	p	Coef.	SE	T-ratio	p	Coef.	SE	T-ratio	p
For Intercept (β_{0j})												
Intercept (γ_{00})	.2196	.0245	8.96	.000	.2168	.0240	9.05	.000	.1828	.0205	8.90	.000
Acres (γ_{01})					.0005	.0001	3.51	.001	.0027	.0005	5.10	.000
For Party slope (β_{1j})												
Party (γ_{10})	.4804	.0220	21.87	.000	.4793	.0220	21.84	.000	.5066	.0215	23.53	.000
Acres (γ_{11})									−.0016	.0004	3.60	.001
For Money slope (β_{2j})												
Money (γ_{20})	.0046	.0004	11.18	.000	.0045	.0005	8.18	.000	.0049	.0005	8.80	.000
Acres (γ_{21})									−.00002	.0000	5.50	.000

Random Effects	Model 1				Model 2				Model 3			
	Std. Dev.	Var. Comp.	χ^2	p	Std. Dev.	Var. Comp.	χ^2	p	Std. Dev.	Var. Comp.	χ^2	p
Intercept (u_{0j}) Party	.1366	.0187	122.0	.000	.1310	.0172	111.4	.000	.0978	.0096	84.1	.000
slope (u_{1j}) Money	.0897	.0080	67.0	.002	.0900	.0081	67.1	.002	.0705	.0050	54.8	.023
slope (u_{2j})	.0012	.0000	36.8	> .50	.0014	.0000	36.0	> .50	.0009	.0000	29.2	> .50
Level-1 (e_{ij})	.1638	.0268			.1636	.0268			.1628	.0265		

Model Fit	Deviance	Parameters	AIC	BIC	Deviance	Parameters	AIC	BIC	Deviance	Parameters	AIC	BIC
	−332.0	10	−312	−269.3	−334.5	11	−312.5	−265.5	−353.8	13	−327.8	−272.3

31

the significance of fixed-effect parameters (Hox, 2002). The Wald Test is interpreted as a Z-statistic from a standard normal distribution. The Wald Z-test is similarly used for testing variance components in multilevel software other than HLM. HLM, assuming that variances may not be normally distributed, instead uses a chi-square test of the residuals. One should be cautious in interpreting any significance tests of variance components. First, variances are bounded at zero, so their distributions are not normal. More importantly, it is not clear exactly what the meaning of a significant variance component should be—after all, we generally expect variances to be non-zero. Thus, variances are like effect-size statistics; one can perform a significance test or form confidence intervals, but it is usually more fruitful to interpret their sizes rather than their significance. (This line of reasoning is why *nlme* does not provide standard errors or significance tests for the variance components in R and S-Plus.)

Examination of Table 2.9 shows that political party and PAC contributions are highly significant level-1 predictors ($p < .001$) for all three models. The intercept model (Model 2) shows that tobacco acreage is also significant, although the effect appears to be rather small—for every additional 1,000 acres of tobacco harvested in a state, we would expect to see an increase in pro-tobacco voting of about .05%.

The slopes model (Model 3) provides a more complex picture of the effects of party, money, and tobacco economy. The results of this model show that tobacco acreage not only significantly affects the average voting level in a state (the intercept effect), but there are also highly significant cross-level interactions. The negative coefficients for the two interactions indicate that the presence of tobacco farming in a state acts to reduce or 'dampen' the effects of being Republican, on the one hand, and receiving tobacco industry money on the other. Another interesting outcome of this analysis is that by including the cross-level interactions, the intercept effect has become much larger—.0027 compared to .0005, over a five-fold increase.

Sometimes, it can be difficult to correctly trace all the effects in a complex multilevel model. It can be useful to plot simple prediction equations based on the estimated parameters. As an example, Figure 2.5 shows the expected voting percentages for Democratic legislators for three different levels of tobacco acreage. The solid line at the bottom shows the relationship of tobacco industry money on voting in a state such as Illinois, where there is no tobacco farming. The dashed line in the middle shows the same relation-ship for a state such as Georgia, which has a moderate amount of tobacco

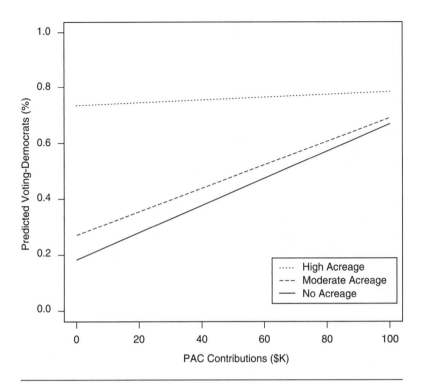

Figure 2.5   Predicted Pro-Tobacco Voting Percent for Democrats by
Amount of Tobacco Acreage

farming (33,000 acres in 1999). Finally, the dotted line at the top shows an
extreme case from North Carolina, with more than 200,000 acres of tobacco
harvested. This figure shows that, in general, the more money accepted
by Democratic legislators, the more likely they are to vote pro-tobacco.
However, this figure shows that the state tobacco economy mediates this
relationship. States with more tobacco acreage are likely to show higher
pro-tobacco voting rates (higher intercepts), but at the same time, the effect
of contributions to individual legislators is lessened (shallower slopes).

Assessing Model Fit–Deviance and R^2

Another important aspect of model specification and testing is examining
how closely the model fits the data. One of the products of a model fit using
ML is the *likelihood* statistic. In fact, the likelihood is what is minimized

in ML estimation of multilevel models. A transformation of the likelihood called the *deviance* is obtained by multiplying the natural log of the likelihood by minus two ($-2LL$). The deviance is a measure of the lack of fit between the data and the model. The deviance for any one model cannot be interpreted directly, but it can be used to compare multiple models to one another. This model comparison can be done between two models fit to the same data set, where one of the models is a subset (has fewer parameters) of the other. The difference of the deviances from each model is distributed as a chi-square statistic with degrees of freedom equal to the difference in the number of parameters estimated in each model.

For example, consider Table 2.9. The deviance for Model 1 is -332. The deviance for Model 2 is -334.5. A lower deviance always implies better fit, and with nested models, the model with more parameters will always have a lower deviance. The difference between the two deviances is 2.5, which is compared to a chi-squared distribution with 1 (11 parameters $-$ 10 parameters) df. The difference is not significant ($p = .114$), so there is no evidence that Model 2 provides a better fit to the data than Model 1. However, the level-2 slopes model (Model 3) *is* significantly better: ($353.8 - 332 = 21.8$, $df = 3$, $p < .001$). So, if we are going to use amount of tobacco acreage as a level-2 predictor, then these results suggest that tobacco acreage be used to predict slopes as well as intercepts of the level-1 predictors.

One disadvantage of the deviance ($-2LL$) is that a model fit to the same data with more parameters will always have smaller deviance. Smaller deviance is good, in that we want to maximize the fit of the model to the data. However, we also generally want to have models that are parsimonious, or able to explain the data with as few parameters as possible. Two other fit indexes have been developed that are based on the deviance but incorporate penalties for a greater number of parameters: the Akaike Information Criterion (AIC) and Schwarz's Bayesian Information Criterion (BIC) (Akaike, 1987; Schwarz, 1978). HLM does not provide AIC or BIC, but they can be calculated easily using Equation 2.11:

Equation 2.11

$$AIC = -2LL + 2p$$

$$BIC = -2LL + p \ln(N)$$

where p is the number of parameters in the model and N is the sample size. The BIC was not developed with multilevel models in mind, so it is not totally clear which sample size should be used. Singer and Willett (2003) suggest that the level-1 sample size should be used, and we follow their advice. As with the deviance, lower AIC or BIC indicates a better model. One advantage that AIC and BIC have is that they can be used to compare two non-nested models. Examination of the AIC and BIC values in Table 2.9 confirms our earlier decision to choose Model 3 as the best model. Model 3 has the lowest values for both AIC and BIC.

In regular OLS regression, the fit of a model is typically assessed by calculating R^2 and interpreting it as the percentage of variance of the outcome accounted for by the predictors in the model. In multilevel modeling, the use of R^2 is more complicated for at least two reasons. First, there is a separate R^2 for each level of the multilevel model. Second, in multilevel models using traditional approaches to calculating R^2, it is possible to run into situations where adding additional predictors results in smaller or even negative values of R^2. This is clearly undesirable. However, based on the work of Snijders and Bosker (1994, 1999), we can utilize an approach that is relatively straightforward to calculate and yields interpretable measures of R^2 for each level.

Instead of interpreting R^2 as a simple percentage of variance accounted for, we will interpret R^2 in a multilevel model as the proportional reduction of prediction error. Given that residuals in a model indicate lack of fit between a model and the data, a better fitting model is one where the residuals are smaller than those in another comparison model. In a two-level model, then, we will have two ways to assess the model fit. First, for level-1, R_1^2 will assess the proportional reduction of error for predicting an individual outcome. Then, for level-2, R_2^2 will assess the proportional reduction of error for predicting a group (level-2 unit) mean.

These statistics are relatively easy to calculate using the output from a fitted model. First, for level-1 our starting point is the variance of the level-1 residuals:

Equation 2.12

$$\text{var(residuals)}_1 = \sigma_r^2 + \sigma_{u_0}^2.$$

Next, we calculate our estimate of this variance for two models: a baseline model and a comparison model. The baseline model is often a null or fully unconstrained model with no level-1 or level-2 predictors. The proportional reduction of prediction error for level-1 is then:

Equation 2.13

$$R_1^2 = 1 - \frac{(\hat{\sigma}_r^2 + \hat{\sigma}_{u_0}^2)_{\text{Comparison}}}{(\hat{\sigma}_r^2 + \hat{\sigma}_{u_0}^2)_{\text{Baseline}}}$$

If the comparison model is a better fit to the data, then the variance of the level-1 residuals will be smaller, leading to a larger R_1^2.

The process for level-2 is similar. First, we start with the formula for the variances of the level-2 residuals:

Equation 2.14

$$\text{var(residuals)}_2 = \frac{\sigma_r^2}{n} + \sigma_{u_0}^2$$

where n is the expected number of level-1 units in each level-2 unit in the population. We calculate sample-based estimates of this variance for the baseline and comparison models and compute the level-2 proportional reduction of prediction error:

Equation 2.15

$$R_2^2 = 1 - \frac{(\hat{\sigma}_r^2/\tilde{n} + \hat{\sigma}_{u_0}^2)_{\text{Comparison}}}{(\hat{\sigma}_r^2/\tilde{n} + \hat{\sigma}_{u_0}^2)_{\text{Baseline}}}$$

Here again, $\hat{\sigma}_r^2$ and $\hat{\sigma}_{u_0}^2$ are provided as part of the basic output from a multilevel model. However, the user will have to provide a value for $\tilde{n}$, which should be the typical number of level-1 units in any level-2 unit. This value can come from theory or from the expectation of what the sample size should be in the population. Lacking theoretical guidance, and if there are varying group sizes in the data set, then one can use the harmonic mean of the level-2 unit sample sizes:

Equation 2.16

$$H = \frac{k}{\sum_1^k (1/n_j)},$$

where k = the number of level-2 units. If the sample sizes of the level-2 units are not too unbalanced, then the simple mean of the group sizes will be close to the harmonic mean and can be used instead.

TABLE 2.10
Values Used to Calculate R_1^2 and R_2^2

Model	$\hat{\sigma}_r^2$	$\hat{\sigma}_{u_0}^2$	H
Baseline: Fully unconstrained	.093	.035	6.23
Comparison: Level-2 slopes	.028	.005	6.23

The only wrinkle to this procedure for calculating R_1^2 and R_2^2 is handling a slopes-as-outcomes model. In a slopes model, in addition to the level-2 variability for the intercept ($\sigma_{u_0}^2$), there will also be a variance for each of the slopes: ($\sigma_{u_1}^2$), ($\sigma_{u_2}^2$), and so on. However, the above equations use only the intercept variability. How should the slope variabilities be handled for R_1^2 and R_2^2? Snijders and Bosker (1999) suggest that the model should be refit without the random slopes. This will result in only the two variance components that are required for the calculations, and usually does not change the actual parameter estimates very much.

Turning to the tobacco voting example, we would like to see how good our final level-2 slopes model (Model 3) is at predicting individual voting behavior and state-level average voting behavior. Table 2.10 presents the estimated variance components and harmonic means needed for the calculations. (Following Snijders & Bosker's recommendations described above, we reran the slopes model with the *Party* and *Money* slopes as fixed rather than random. This results in the model having only two variance components estimates: $\hat{\sigma}_r^2$ and $\hat{\sigma}_{u_0}^2$.)

Using these data, R_1^2 is $[(1 - (.028 + .005)/(.093 + .035)]) = .742$. For level-2, R_2^2 is $1 - \frac{(.028/6.23 + .005)}{(.093/6.23 + .035)} = .81$. So, by including two level-1 predictors (*Party* and *Money*) and one level-2 two predictor (*Acres*), we are able to improve the predictive ability of the model compared to a null model by approximately 75% to 80%.

Evaluating the Model: Diagnostics

An important part of determining the adequacy of a multilevel model is checking whether the underlying assumptions of the model appear valid for the data. Two of the most important assumptions that can be empirically checked in a multilevel model are: (a) that the level-1 (within-group) errors are independent and normally distributed with a mean of zero; and (b) that the random effects are normally distributed with a mean of zero, and are independent across groups. These assumptions can be assessed using the level-1 and level-2 residuals produced during the modeling process. (Although the graphical residual analysis techniques discussed here can be done with any major statistical package, the *lme* and *nlme* procedures in S-Plus or R make the process especially easy and flexible. Residuals from the multilevel models are stored in model fit objects, and these objects can be used by graphing procedures that automatically know how to treat residuals. See Pinheiro & Bates (2000) for extensive discussion and examples.)

We first turn to examination of the level-1 residuals. For this section, we will focus on our final model (Model 3 in Table 2.9.). A potentially useful residual plot to consider is the boxplot of residuals by state (Figure 2.6). This plot can be used to determine if the residuals are centered at 0 (the vertical line), and that the variances are constant across groups. The residuals do seem to be centered at 0, albeit with a fair amount of variability. It does appear that variability is not constant across states. However, many of the states have very small sample sizes, so we cannot rely too heavily on the individual boxplots for assessment of the within-group variances. (It appears that there is a pattern of residuals where states at the top of the graph have positive residuals, whereas the states at the bottom show primarily negative residuals. This is an artifact of the ordering of the states, where S-Plus orders the states from top to bottom by largest value of the dependent variable, Voting %.)

Another common diagnostic plot is a scatter plot of standardized residuals against fitted values. This is particularly useful to assess problems with heteroscedasticity. Figure 2.7 shows the standardized residuals by political party. The most noticeable pattern is the straight-edge diagonal seen in the bottom left of the Democrats and the top right of the Republicans. This is an indication of both a floor-effect (many Democrats always vote against the industry, and Voting % cannot be less than zero) and a ceiling effect (many Republican always vote for the industry, and Voting % cannot be greater than 1). Floor and ceiling effects are not fatal flaws in a model, but we shall see in the first section of Chapter 3 how to build a model that avoids this problem with the data. The residuals appear to be centered at 0, and there do not appear to be major problems with heteroscedasticity. Furthermore, the

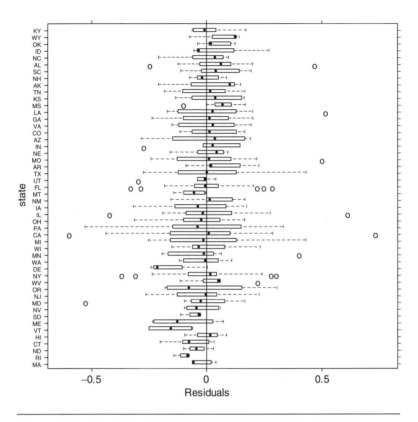

Figure 2.6 Boxplots of the Within-State Residuals for Model 3

variability of the residuals seems to be roughly the same for both parties. Finally, a number of outlying values are marked by the state from which they come. These data points are senators and representatives who tended to vote "against their party," and thus do not seem to fit the model well. The most interesting point about these outliers is that they tend to come from the larger states.

The final plot to consider for the level-1 residuals is a normal quantile-quantile plot, or QQ-plot (Cleveland, 1993). As the name suggests, a normal QQ-plot can be used to assess the normality of a data set. If the data being plotted are normally distributed, they will be arrayed along a straight line in the QQ-plot. Figure 2.8 shows that for our tobacco voting data, the level-1 residuals are quite normal. There are a few extreme points at the upper end

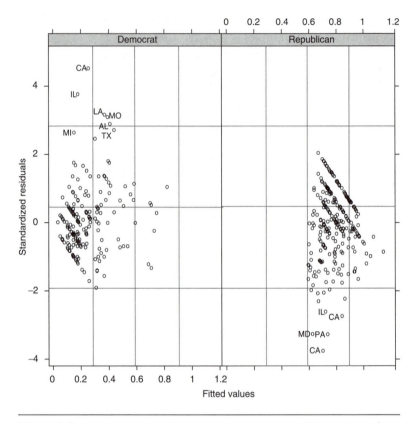

Figure 2.7   Scatterplot of Standardized Residuals by Fitted Values for
Model 3 by Party

of the Democrats and the lower end of the Republicans that do not follow the
normal distribution. These points, in fact, correspond to the same outliers
seen in Figure 2.7.

The same types of plots can be used to check the level-2, random-effects
assumptions. The random effects are also assumed to be normally distributed
with zero mean. Because our model has three random effects (intercept,
Money slope, and Party slope), we will need to check each of them. Figure 2.9
shows a set of QQ-plots for each of the random effects. The effects for Party
appear to be the closest to normal. The lines are not as smooth as before,
because there are only 50 level-2 residuals, whereas there were 527 level-1
residuals.

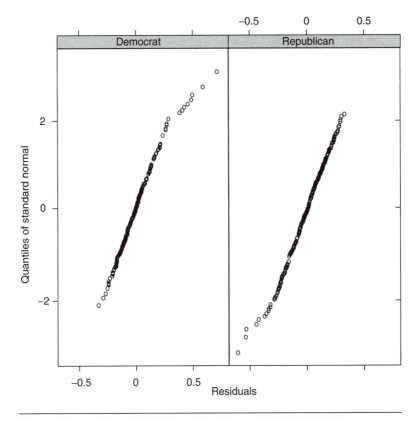

Figure 2.8   Normal QQ-plot of Residuals of Model 3 by Party

Finally, a scatter plot matrix can be used again to check to see where the random effects are centered. Also, we can determine if the random effects are independent of one another across the groups. Figure 2.10 presents a scatter plot matrix for the three random effects. The effects do appear to be centered at zero and there does not appear to be a major problem of heteroscedasticity. However, there appears to be a moderately large negative correlation between the intercept and both Money and Party. Money and Party, on the other hand, do not appear to be related to each other. These correlations may be another by-product of the floor and ceiling effects.

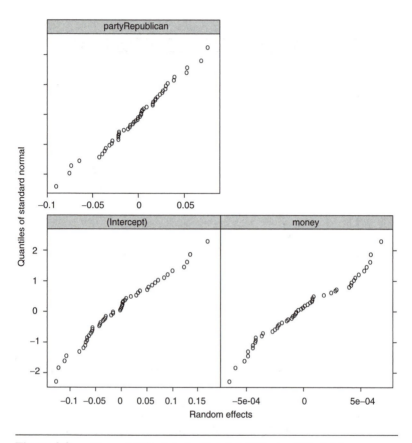

Figure 2.9   Normal QQ-plots for Random Effects of Model 3

In addition to the approaches described above, there are other diagnostics that the user may be interested in examining. In particular, it is often fruitful to examine influence statistics for level-2 units in a multilevel model. The steps for doing this are beyond the scope of this monograph, but Snijders and Bosker (1999, Chapter 9) outline the procedure. Also, a macro for calculating the level-2 influence statistics in MLwiN is available at http://stat.gamma.rug.nl/snijders/mlnmac.htm.

Prediction: Posterior Means

Although much of the time we are most interested in the estimation of the fixed part of a multilevel model, there are a number of reasons why we might

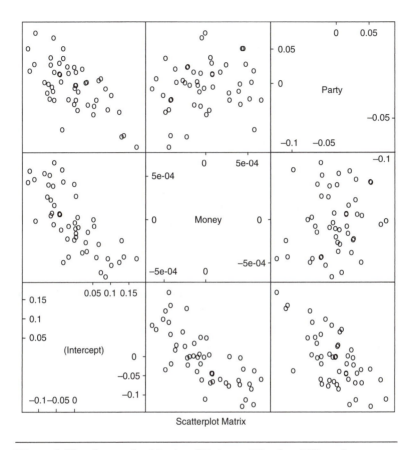

Figure 2.10   Scatterplot Matrix of Estimated Random Effects for
Model 3

want to examine the random part, in particular to explore in more detail the
variability between level-2 units on the intercepts and slopes of the level-1
model. The procedure to do this is known as empirical Bayes estimation
(Armitage & Colton, 1998).

Consider the fully unconstrained model listed at the top of Table 2.1. γ_{00}
is the fixed effect that determines the intercept, and is simply the grand mean
of Y_{ij}. However, u_{0j} tells us that groups vary around that grand mean. If we
want to estimate β_{0j} for a particular level-2 unit, we could simply calculate
$\bar{Y}_{.j}$, the mean for the particular group. This is the same value that you would
get if you simply performed an OLS regression for that particular group

by itself. However, we would trust this as an estimate for the particular group only if Y were measured with no error. Moreover, the less reliable our measure of Y is in a particular group, the more we will want to use the grand mean across all of the groups as our estimate. This is essentially how the empirical Bayes estimate works:

Equation 2.17

$$\hat{\beta}_{0j}^{EB} = \lambda_j \hat{\beta}_{0j}^{OLS} + (1 - \lambda_j)\hat{\gamma}_{00},$$

where λ_j is the reliability of Y in group j. If the reliability is high (close to 1), then the Bayesian estimate of the intercept will be very close to the simple OLS estimate from the individual group. If the reliability is low, then the Bayesian estimate will approach the fitted value for the grand mean of Y. (Remember that $\hat{\gamma}_{00}$ is our estimate of the grand mean of Y.) Note that the Bayesian estimate will always lie between the group mean and the grand mean, and, as reliability worsens, the estimate will "shrink" toward the grand mean. Thus, EB estimates are sometimes called "*shrinkage estimates.*" Thus, the Bayesian estimate of the multilevel regression parameters represents a balance between the information obtained from a specific group and information obtained from the entire data set.

The formula for the reliability,

Equation 2.18

$$\lambda_j = \frac{\sigma_{u_0}^2}{(\sigma_{u_0}^2 + \sigma_r^2/n_j)},$$

indicates that the major determinant of high reliability for a particular group is the number of level-1 units in that group (n_j). This makes sense in that a group with a relatively large sample size is contributing more information to the model than a group that only has only a small number of members. In our example, California will have a more reliable estimate of voting percentage (with 55 members of Congress) than will Oregon (with only 7).

Table 2.11 lists the empirical Bayes estimates for each state for Model 3. The table also displays the number of legislators in each state and the amount of harvested acres of tobacco. By examining these numbers, you can see that those states with the smallest sample size and with no tobacco acreage tend to have EB estimates that are closest to the fitted gammas, thus demonstrating Equation 2.17. For example, consider the EB estimates

TABLE 2.11
Empirical Bayes Estimates for 50 States (based on Model 3)

State	Legislators	EB-Intercept	EB-Party	EB-Money	Tobacco Acres (Thousands)
AK	3	.1937	.5086	.0048	0.0
AL	9	.3660	.4168	.0039	0.0
AR	5	.2824	.4753	.0041	0.0
AZ	8	.1969	.4986	.0048	0.0
CA	55	.1570	.5646	.0046	0.0
CO	8	.2086	.5370	.0043	0.0
CT	8	.0664	.5201	.0060	3.0
DE	3	.1107	.4915	.0058	0.0
FL	25	.2054	.4755	.0049	5.8
GA	13	.2322	.4891	.0042	33.0
HI	4	.1873	.5042	.0049	0.0
IA	7	.1241	.4788	.0058	0.0
ID	3	.2249	.5148	.0043	0.0
IL	21	.1901	.5304	.0046	0.0
IN	11	.2731	.5086	.0038	6.5
KS	6	.2518	.4880	.0043	0.0
KY	7	.8259	.1243	.0001	221.6
LA	10	.2943	.4969	.0038	0.0
MA	12	.0595	.5557	.0057	1.3
MD	10	.1177	.4976	.0056	6.5
ME	4	.1135	.4806	.0059	0.0
MI	18	.1542	.5545	.0047	0.0
MN	10	.1933	.4692	.0052	0.0
MO	11	.3270	.4270	.0042	2.3
MS	7	.3157	.4721	.0038	0.0
MT	3	.1526	.5134	.0052	0.0
NC	13	.6767	.2190	.0008	207.8
ND	3	.1440	.5244	.0051	0.0
NE	5	.1680	.5388	.0047	0.0
NH	4	.1898	.5080	.0048	0.0
NJ	15	.1508	.4354	.0060	0.0
NM	5	.1867	.5385	.0045	0.0
NV	4	.1426	.5247	.0051	0.0

(Continued)

46

TABLE 2.11

(Continued)

State	Legislators	EB-Intercept	EB-Party	EB-Money	Tobacco Acres (Thousands)
NY	32	.0753	.5879	.0052	0.0
OH	20	.1483	.4849	.0054	9.8
OK	8	.2645	.5226	.0038	0.0
OR	7	.1701	.5270	.0048	0.0
PA	23	.1855	.4767	.0051	6.2
RI	4	.0714	.5349	.0058	0.0
SC	8	.3874	.4420	.0030	39.0
SD	3	.1278	.5262	.0053	0.0
TN	11	.3553	.3736	.0039	63.2
TX	32	.3256	.4367	.0041	0.0
UT	5	.1247	.4953	.0057	0.0
VA	12	.3440	.4013	.0039	38.3
VT	2	.1108	.5055	.0057	0.0
WA	11	.1185	.5369	.0053	0.0
WI	11	.1309	.5792	.0047	1.2
WV	5	.2445	.4729	.0046	1.6
WY	3	.2203	.5140	.0044	0.0

for Alaska (EB-Intercept = .19, EB-Party = .51, EB-Money = .0048) and for New York (EB-Intercept = .08, EB-Party = .59, EB-Money = .0052), and compare each of these to the general estimates taken from Model 3 (Intercept = .18, Party = .51, Money = .0049). Alaska, with only three members of Congress, has a much lower reliability of its estimates; therefore, the EB estimates for Alaska are close to the overall Model 3 estimates. New York, on the other hand, has a sample size of 32. With its higher reliability, New York's Bayesian estimates are relatively further away from the general model estimates.

Typically, these EB estimates are used in one of two ways. First, the shrinkage estimates can be used to examine or identify individual level-2 units of interest. For example, perusing Table 2.11, we can quickly ascertain the state with the highest intercept (KY) or the states that show the strongest relationship between money and pro-tobacco voting (CT and NJ).

47

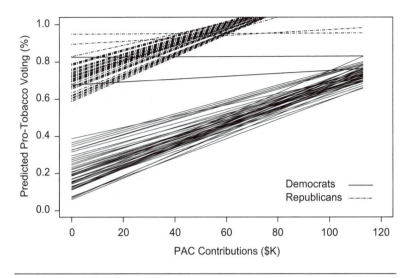

Figure 2.11   Bayesian Estimated Regression Lines for Model 3 by *Party*

The second use is to examine all of the EB prediction equations to explore the variability of the individual state models. Figure 2.11 plots the prediction equations for each state, with separate lines for Democrats and Republicans. The figure clearly shows the strong effect for political party, and the consistent positive effect of money on pro-tobacco voting. The figure shows that most states fall within a fairly tight range, with Republicans showing less variability than Democrats, especially with larger amounts of money. The small number of lines that appear to be outliers are identified as the states with large tobacco economies.

Another way to use the EB prediction equations is to see how they fit to the original data. Figure 2.12 shows a trellis plot of each state's data with the shrinkage estimates. Party is ignored for this graph. This graph is useful to see which states have prediction equations that lie close to the original data. In general, states with larger sample sizes and more variability on Money and Voting % show greater agreement between the data and the predictions. So, states such as Virginia and Ohio show a better match between their data and the Bayesian prediction estimates than a state such as Oregon (which had no members of Congress who accepted any tobacco industry PAC money).

48

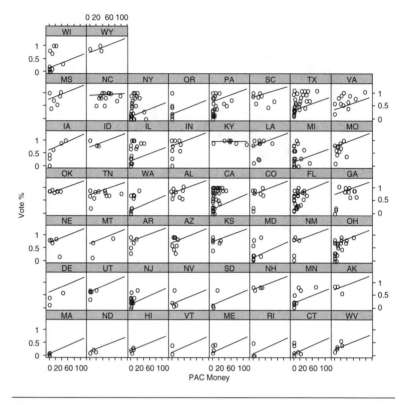

Figure 2.12   Scatterplots of Data with Empirical Bayes Prediction Estimates

Centering

An important issue in multilevel modeling that we have ignored until now is that of centering level-1 predictor variables. Centering is simply the process of linearly transforming a variable X by subtracting a meaningful constant, often some type of mean of X. For example, consider centering X on its grand mean:

Equation 2.19

$$X'_{ij} = (X_{ij} - \bar{X}_{..}).$$

X'_{ij} is now interpreted as a deviation away from the grand mean, rather than a raw score. For example, if we perform grand-mean centering on

Money, it is now interpreted as how much more or less PAC money an individual member of Congress receives compared to the average for all members of Congress members. Furthermore, a score of 0 on the transformed variable is now interpreted as receiving the average amount of money from the tobacco industry. This may be a more meaningful reference point than the untransformed variable, where 0 represents a person who received no money from the industry.

In fact, an important use of centering is to come up with a meaningful 0-point for a predictor variable. Centering (sometimes called *reparameterization*) is often done in ordinary multiple regression. However, centering is not a major issue in ordinary regression because the important elements of a multiple regression model (e.g., parameter estimates, standard errors, model fit, etc.) are not changed when a predictor variable is centered.

This is not the case for multilevel modeling. If a multilevel model has random slopes, then centering a level-1 predictor variable can change some elements of the model (and not just the interpretation of the transformed variable.). To see why this is so, consider Figure 2.13 (adapted from Hox, 2002). This figure shows an example where the slopes of Y on X vary across groups. This would suggest the need for a random-slopes multilevel model. Two zero-points on the x-axis are highlighted. One is the zero-point for the original X variable, whereas the other (X^*) is the shifted zero-point for some centered version of X. Notice that the variability of the intercepts of the regression lines is different at these two points; it is larger for X^* than it is for X. This tells us that the variance of the level-1 intercept is not constant, and will change if we center X. If we did not fit a random-slopes model, then the slopes of the three lines would be the same and the variance would not change when centering X (see Figure 2.1).

Table 2.12 shows how this works for the tobacco data. The left side of the table presents our final model from before (Model 3), where neither of the level-one predictors are centered. That is, a 0 for money means that that legislator received no money from a tobacco PAC source. Remember that we interpret the parameter coefficient for the intercept as the expected value when all the predictors are zero. In this case, we predict that a Democrat who receives *no* PAC money (Party = 0 and Money = 0) will vote pro-tobacco 18.3% of the time. The middle part of the table shows the results for the same model, except that Money has now been grand-mean centered. The estimate for the intercept has now changed to .246. We interpret this differently because of the centered Money predictor. Now we say that a Democrat who

50

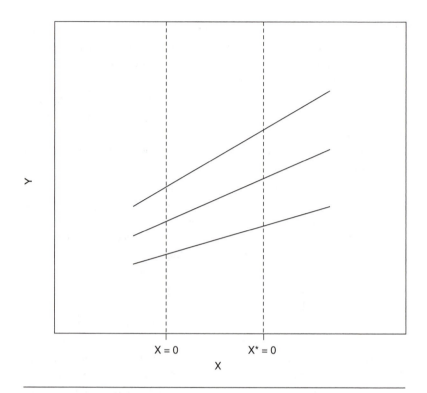

X = 0   X* = 0

X

Figure 2.13   Example Showing Varying Intercept Variability
Due to Centering

receives the *average* amount of money for Congress will vote pro-tobacco
approximately 25% of the time. Notice that the only parts of the model
that have changed are those parameter estimates and variance components
associated with the intercept. The slopes and variance components for Money
and Party are unaffected, as is the overall fit of the model.

There is another common way to center a level-1 predictor. Instead of
adjusting by the grand mean, we can adjust for the group mean:

Equation 2.20

$$X'_{ij} = (X_{ij} - \bar{X}_{.j}).$$

A group-centered variable is interpreted as a deviation away from the mean
within a particular group. Group-mean centering is much more complicated

TABLE 2.12
Comparison of Centered and Noncentered Models

Fixed Effects	Not Centered (0 = No PAC money received)		Grand-Mean Centered (0 = Avg. amount of PAC money received across all states)		Group-Mean Centered (0 = Avg. amount of PAC money received within a particular state)	
	Coef.	SE	Coef.	SE	Coef.	SE
For Intercept (β_{0j})						
Intercept (γ_{00})	.1828	.0205	.2461	.0198	.2305	.0224
Acres (γ_{01})	.0027	.0005	.0024	.0005	.0028	.0005
For Party slope (β_{1j})						
Party (γ_{10})	.5066	.0215	.5066	.0215	.5120	.0213
Acres (γ_{11})	−.0016	.0004	−.0016	.0004	−.0017	.0005
For Money slope (β_{2j})						
Money (γ_{20})	.0049	.0005	.0049	.0005	.0044	.0006
Acres (γ_{21})	−.00002	.0000	−.00002	.0000	−.00002	.0000
Random Effects	Std. Dev.	Var. Comp.	Std. Dev.	Var. Comp.	Std. Dev.	Var. Comp.
Intercept (u_{0j})	.098	.010	.090	.008	.115	.013
Party slope (u_{1j})	.070	.005	.070	.005	.069	.005
Money slope (u_{2j})	.001	.000	.001	.000	.000	.000
Level-1 (e_{ij})	.163	.026	.163	.026	.163	.027
Model Fit	Deviance	Parameters	Deviance	Parameters	Deviance	Parameters
	−353.8	13	−353.8	13	−335.6	13

52

than centering with the grand mean. Not only are the interpretations more difficult, but the effects on the multilevel model are more pervasive. This can be seen in the right side of Table 2.12. Now we interpret the intercept as indicating that a Democrat who receives the average amount of PAC money received *in his or her state,* is likely to vote pro-tobacco 23% of the time. Notice that unlike grand-mean centering, group-mean centering has resulted in different parameter and variance estimates throughout the entire model. In our example, they are not that different, but in other research situations, that may not be the case. Given these complexities, one should use group-mean centering only if there are strong theoretical reasons to do so. One type of research situation is when you want to be able to distinguish between within-group and between-group regressions. This is often the case in growth curve modeling using longitudinal data (see below). Another research area where group-mean centering is useful is when you are interested in "frog-pond" effects, where the interest is more in the fit of an individual to his or her environment rather than on how individual scores affect some outcome (Hox, 2002).

Centering in multilevel modeling can be confusing, and there is still a lot of debate in the literature about the merits of various centering approaches. For more detailed discussions of these issues, see a useful series of papers presented in the *Multilevel Modelling Newsletter* [*sic*] (Kreft, 1995; Longford, 1989; Plewis, 1989; Raudenbush, 1989), available online at http://multilevel.ioe.ac.uk/publref/newsletters.html. The following guidelines about centering may be helpful for the practitioner:

1. Always base centering decisions on theoretical grounds. Although centering can have statistical consequences, these should be of secondary concern compared to the scientific goals of the analyses.
2. If any of the predictor variables do not have meaningful zero-points, they should be centered so that the intercepts in the multilevel model will be interpretable. For example, a Likert-type variable scored from 1 to 7 should not be used in its raw form. If it were, then the intercept would be interpreted as the expected value when the scale is 0, which is an impossible value.
3. Binary or indicator variables can also be centered. By adjusting for the grand-mean of a binary variable, you are, in effect, removing the effects of that variable when interpreting the intercept. For example, by centering on Party and Money in the tobacco data set, the

resulting intercept estimate is .51. This indicates that a typical legislator, regardless of political party, votes pro-tobacco about half of the time.

4. Grand-mean centering of a level-1 predictor affects only the parts of the model associated with the intercept.

5. Group-mean centering can be useful in certain situations, but it should be employed only when necessary.

3. EXTENDING THE BASIC MULTILEVEL MODEL

Using Generalized Multilevel Modeling

As suggested above, there is an important limitation in modeling the congressional voting behavior with the basic hierarchical linear model. Our dependent variable is a proportion, and thus violates the general linear model assumptions of normality and homoscedastic errors. Also, because the voting proportion is bounded at 0 and 1, we may find that predictions of voting behavior based on the fitted models lead to estimated values outside of that range. It is difficult to know what to make of a prediction that says a particular type of Congress member will vote pro-tobacco 120% of the time!

Fortunately, multilevel modeling can be extended to handle a wide variety of different types of non-continuous or non-normal dependent variables, including binary, proportion, count, and ordinal variables. To do this, we use what is called a *generalized* hierarchical linear model (GHLM). GHLM works by including a necessary transformation and an appropriate error distribution for the dependent variable into the statistical model.

As an example, consider a binary (dichotomous) dependent variable. This untransformed variable is bounded by 0 and 1 and is highly non-normal. We can assume that the underlying probability distribution is binomial with mean μ. Our estimate of μ is p, which we interpret as the probability of the event occurring. A typical transformation for a binomial model is the logit:

Equation 3.1

$$\text{logit}(p) = \ln\left(\frac{p}{1-p}\right).$$

54

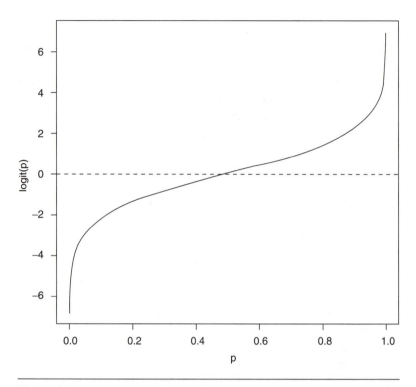

Figure 3.1   Illustration of Logit Transformation

Figure 3.1 illustrates why the logit transformation is so useful. Although p is bounded, the logit of p is unbounded, and the density of logit(p) is much closer to normal.

In GHLM, this type of transformation is called a *link function*. First, we set up a transformational link that connects the untransformed dependent variable Y, to a new transformed variable η. So, in the case of binary data, our link function is:

Equation 3.2

$$\eta = \text{logit}(Y).$$

TABLE 3.1
Canonical Link Functions for GHLM

Dependent Variable	Link Function	Formula	Probability Distribution
Binary	Logit	$\eta = \ln(\frac{Y}{1-Y})$	Binomial
Proportion	Logit	$\eta = \ln(\frac{Y}{1-Y})$	Binomial
Count	Log	$\eta = \ln(Y)$	Poisson
Ordinal	Cumulative logit	See Raudenbush and Bryk (2002), p. 319	Multinomial

NOTE: Adapted from Raudenbush and Bryk (2002), Table 10.8, p. 333.

We then set up a traditional level-1 prediction model as described in Chapter 2:

Equation 3.3

$$\eta = \beta_0 + \beta_1 X_1 + \cdots + \beta_k X_k$$

for k predictor variables. Notice that there is no term for the level-1 error variance. For binary (and binomial) variables, the variance is completely determined by the mean, and thus is not a separate term to be estimated. Level-2 models that predict the level-1 betas can then be constructed as before.

There are certain link functions and associated probability distributions that are typically used for the various types of non-normal data. These so-called *canonical* link functions are listed in Table 3.1 (Raudenbush & Bryk, 2002). One of the advantages of GHLM is that you can explicitly pick alternative link functions and/or probability distributions that are appropriate for your data and theories.

We can see how GHLM works by applying it to our tobacco voting data. In Chapter 2, we built a model that predicted the proportion of the total votes that were in the pro-tobacco industry direction. However, this proportion was actually obtained by aggregating across the set of individual votes in which a member of Congress participated during the 105th and 106th Congresses (from 1997 to 2000). So, instead of aggregating to obtain a proportion, we can instead use GHLM to build a model that predicts the likelihood of voting pro-tobacco for any *individual* bill or amendment.

In this model, the dependent variable Vote is binary, and is coded 0 for a vote that was against the tobacco industry, and coded 1 for a pro-industry vote. We still wish to build a multilevel model, but now the levels have changed. At level-1, we are measuring and predicting votes on individual bills. These individual votes are nested within a particular member of Congress, so level-2 is now the individual. We wish to model the likelihood of voting pro-tobacco on any individual bill. This can be seen more explicitly with the formal model:

Equation 3.4

$$\text{Level 1:} \quad \eta_{ij} = \text{logit}(Y_{ij})$$
$$\eta_{ij} = \pi_{0j}$$
$$\text{Level 2:} \quad \pi_{0j} = \beta_{00} + \beta_{01}\text{Party}_j + \beta_{02}\text{Money}_j + u_{0j}$$

with the logit link function specified, and where Y_{ij} is the vote of the jth member of Congress on the ith bill. The only predictors in this model are the level-2 individual predictors of political party and amount of PAC money received. If we had relevant bill level predictors (such as whether the vote was for a full bill or just an amendment, or which party sponsored the bill), then they could be included in the level-1 submodel. In this case, we are modeling only the level-1 intercept, which is interpreted as the average probability that an individual member of Congress would vote pro-tobacco on a bill. Notice again that there is no error term for the level-1 submodel. This model also has only one random effect, which is the variability of the individual votes across persons (u_{0j}).

Table 3.2 presents the results of the GHLM of the binary voting data. As before, all of the coefficients are significant. However, before their values can be interpreted correctly, the coefficients need to be transformed back into their original underlying units. This is done by using the appropriate inverse function of the original link function. The inverse of the logit function is the logistic function:

Equation 3.5

$$Y = \text{logistic}(\beta_0 + \beta_1 X_1 + \beta_2 X_2) = \frac{e^{(\beta_0 + \beta_1 X_1 + \beta_2 X_2)}}{1 + e^{(\beta_0 + \beta_1 X_1 + \beta_2 X_2)}}.$$

So, to find the predicted probability that a Democrat receiving no PAC funds would vote pro-tobacco (Party = 0 and Money = 0), we would

TABLE 3.2

Results of 2-Level GHLM of Binary Voting Data

Fixed Effects	Coef.	SE	T-ratio	p
For Intercept (π_{0j})				
Intercept (β_{00})	-1.721	.0763	22.54	.000
Party (β_{01})	2.544	.0987	25.78	.000
Money (β_{02})	0.0325	.0029	11.36	.000
Random Effects	Std. Dev.	Var. Comp.	χ^2	p
Intercept (u_{0j})	.834	.696	1439.0	.000
Dispersion index	.937			
Model Fit	Deviance	Parameters	AIC	BIC
	7636.8	4	7644.8	7672.5

calculate logistic$(-1.721) = [(e^{-1.721}/(1 + e^{-1.721})]) = .152$. For a Republican who receives no funds (Party $= 1$, Money $= 0$), we calculate logistic$(-1.721 + 2.544)$, which gives the predicted probability of .695. Finally, for a Republican who received \$10,000 (Party $= 1$, Money $= 10$), logistic$(-1.721 + 2.544 + 10 * .0325) = .759$. Notice that these probability values are similar to the results of Model 3 listed in Table 2.9.

It is often easier to interpret the results of a GHLM by plotting the transformed coefficients to get a prediction graph. Figure 3.2 shows the predicted voting probabilities for the Democratic and Republican legislators. This plot also highlights the non-linear nature of the model. In particular, by using a GHLM, we get predictions that make sense and do not go outside the boundaries of a probability.

As noted earlier, a binomial model does not have a separate error-variance term in the first level of the model because the variance is a function of the population mean. However, some software, such as HLM and R/S-Plus, will calculate a 1st-level error variance scaling factor that measures the extent to which the observed errors follow the theoretical binomial error distribution. A scaling factor of 1.00 indicates perfect fit between the observed errors and the theoretical expectation. Values under 1.00 indicate

58

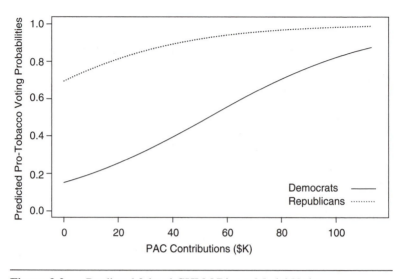

Figure 3.2   Predicted 2-level GHLM Binary Model Voting
Probabilities

underdispersion, and values greater than 1.00 indicate *overdispersion.* Over-
and underdispersion may indicate model misspecification, overly influential
outliers, or the exclusion of an important level in the model. This dispersion
index serves as a good diagnostic for binary/binomial models, and very
large or small values should always lead to careful examination of your
model. The Dispersion Index value of .94 in Table 3.2 indicates minor
underdispersion in our model, probably not large enough to pose a major
problem.

One should be cautious about interpreting the deviance, AIC, and BIC
for GHLM models. GHLM does not estimate models using ML or REML.
Instead, many software packages use a *penalized quasi-likelihood* (PQL)
estimation procedure. PQL produces an asymptotic approximation to the
likelihood. Therefore, the deviance and the information theoretic statistics
such as the AIC, which are based on the deviance, may be less reliable,
especially for small sample sizes. The technical details of PQL and other
non-linear estimation techniques are described in Raudenbush and Bryk
(2002) and Pinheiro and Bates (2000).

Three-Level Models

Up to now, we have considered only two-level models. First, in Chapter 2, we considered voting behavior at the person level influenced by state-level characteristics. Second, in the first Section of Chapter 3, we modeled votes on individual bills influenced by person level characteristics. As discussed in the previous section, there were numerous statistical advantages to modeling the binary voting behavior using GHLM. However, by using only a two-level model which models individual votes as a function of person attributes, we lost the ability to see how these attributes (i.e., Party and Money) were random effects at the state level.

Fortunately, HLM and GHLM can be extended to handle more than two levels. It is not uncommon to come across three-level modeling situations in the social and health sciences. For example, in education, it is common to see data collected at three levels: students nested in classrooms nested in schools. All of the same considerations for building two-level models apply to three-level models; in particular, the hypothesized effects at each level should be clearly defined and appropriately measured.

Although the extension of the two-level statistical model to three levels is relatively straightforward, the specification of the random effects can become confusing. In a two-level model, remember that the level-1 intercepts and slopes may be considered random at level-2. In a three-level model, level-1 intercepts and slopes may be random at level-2 *and* level-3. By random, we mean that the level-1 intercepts and slopes may vary across level-2 units and level-3 units. Suppose, for example, that we are interested in modeling reading achievement by students in various classrooms and schools. We may hypothesize that average reading scores (level-1 intercepts) and the effects of socioeconomic status (SES) on reading scores (level-1 slope) vary across classrooms (level-2) and across schools (level-3).

In addition, any predictors that we include in a level-2 submodel may be considered random at level-3. So, if we include a measure of teacher experience at level-2, the effects of this predictor variable may be hypothesized to vary across schools, and thus will be entered as a random-effect at level-3 in the three-level model. To help clarify this example, Equation 3.6 displays one possible HLM statistical model:

60

Equation 3.6

Level 1: $Y_{ijk} = \pi_{0jk} + \pi_{1jk}(\text{SES})_{ijk} + \varepsilon_{ijk}$

Level 2: $\pi_{0jk} = \beta_{00k} + \beta_{01k}(\text{Exp})_{jk} + r_{0jk}$

$\pi_{1jk} = \beta_{10k} + \beta_{11k}(\text{Exp})_{jk} + r_{1jk}$

Level 3: $\beta_{00k} = \gamma_{000} + u_{00k}$

$\beta_{01k} = \gamma_{010} + u_{01k}$

$\beta_{10k} = \gamma_{100} + u_{10k}$

$\beta_{11k} = \gamma_{110} + u_{11k}$

Here, Y_{ijk} is the reading score for the ith student in the jth class in the kth school. SES is a level-1 predictor, and teacher experience (Exp) is a level-2 predictor. The level-1 and -2 intercepts and slopes are all modeled as random effects. As usual, this set of equations can be reduced to a single mixed-model equation:

Equation 3.7

$$Y_{ijk} = \gamma_{000} + \gamma_{010}(\text{Exp}) + \gamma_{100}(\text{SES}) + \gamma_{110}(\text{Exp})(\text{SES})$$
$$+ u_{00k} + u_{01k}(\text{Exp}) + u_{10k}(\text{SES}) + u_{11k}(\text{Exp})(\text{SES})$$
$$+ r_{0jk} + r_{1jk}(\text{SES}) + \varepsilon_{ijk}.$$

Whereas Equation 3.6 makes it clear that there are three levels in the model with one predictor at level-1 and one predictor at level-2, Equation 3.7 makes it easier to see that this model has four fixed effects and seven variance components (random effects). In particular, there is an important fixed-effect cross-level interaction (γ_{110}) that is easy to miss if you were looking only at Equation 3.6.

Generalized hierarchical linear models (GHLMs) can also be extended to three levels. Our voting data set provides a good example of just such a three-level binary multilevel model. Previously, we have fit two different two-level models to these data: In the first, members of Congress were nested within states; in the second, votes on individual bills were nested within each member of Congress. We can combine these two approaches into a single three-level model where individual votes are nested in members of Congress who are in turn nested within states.

Equation 3.8 presents the formal three-level statistical model. As before, we are using a binomial model with a logit link function. Political party and amount of PAC money received are the predictors at the level of the Congress member (now level-2). Acres is the only level-3 predictor, and this time it is hypothesized to affect only the level-2 intercept and not the level-2 slopes.

Equation 3.8

$$\text{Level 1:} \quad \eta_{ijk} = \text{logit}(Y_{ijk})$$
$$\eta_{ijk} = \pi_{0jk}$$
$$\text{Level 2:} \quad \pi_{0jk} = \beta_{00k} + \beta_{01k}(\text{Party})_{jk}$$
$$+ \beta_{02k}(\text{Money})_{jk} + r_{0jk}$$
$$\text{Level 3:} \quad \beta_{00k} = \gamma_{000} + \gamma_{001}(\text{Acres})_k + u_{00k}$$
$$\beta_{01k} = \gamma_{010} + u_{01k}$$
$$\beta_{02k} = \gamma_{020} + u_{02k}$$

Equation 3.9 shows the single-equation, mixed-model formula, and indicates that our model has four fixed effects and four random effects. Notice that there is no cross-level interaction effect, because Acres is allowed to affect only the intercept.

Equation 3.9

$$Y_{ijk} = \text{logistic} \left(\begin{array}{c} \gamma_{000} + \gamma_{001}(\text{Acres})_k + \gamma_{010}(\text{Party})_{jk} + \gamma_{020}(\text{Money})_{jk} \\ + u_{00k} + u_{01k}(\text{Party})_{jk} + u_{02k}(\text{Money})_{jk} + r_{0jk} \end{array} \right)$$

The results of fitting this model appear in Table 3.3. The results are essentially consistent with the previous models. Party, money, and tobacco acreage are all significant predictors of voting behavior. The effect of money is slightly smaller in the three-level model than in the two-level model, presumably because some of the effects of money are captured by the tobacco economy in a state—legislators from states with tobacco acreage are receiving more money from the tobacco industry than are legislators from states with no tobacco harvest. Figure 3.3 plots the prediction equations for the fitted model, including the effects of three different levels of state tobacco acreage. The shapes of the curves (i.e., the effects of Party and Money) are quite similar to the two-level model. This plot shows us that although tobacco acreage is a significant effect in the model, the effects are not noticeable until acreage is large, on the order of 100,000 acres. Only two states (Kentucky and North Carolina) have a tobacco harvest more than 100,000 acres, so, for most states, only political party and PAC contributions need to be taken into account.

TABLE 3.3
Results of 3-Level GHLM of Binary Voting Data

Fixed Effects	Coef.	SE	T-ratio	p
For Intercept (π_{0jk})				
For Intercept (β_{00k})				
Intercept (γ_{000})	−1.644	.1413	11.62	.000
Acres (γ_{001})	0.0060	.0020	2.96	.005
Party (γ_{010})	2.450	.1144	21.41	.000
Money (γ_{020})	0.0249	.0035	7.04	.000

Random Effects	Std. Dev.	Var. Comp.	χ^2	p
Intercept-1 (r_{0j})	.647	.419	781.7	.000
Intercept-2 (u_{00})	.770	.593	89.7	.000
Slope-Party (u_{01})	.397	.158	47.4	.117
Slope-Money (u_{02})	.011	.000	37.5	.448
Dispersion index	.943			

Model Fit	Deviance	Parameters	AIC	BIC
	7615.8	5	7625.8	7660.4

The other important part of the fitted model is the random effects. In the two-level model, the standard deviation of the person-level random effect is .834. In the three-level model, the person-level variability is now lower (.647), and is, in fact, smaller than the inter-state variability (.770). This tells us that there is as much variability in voting behavior between states as there is between legislators within the states. The random effects of the two person-level slopes are smaller than those for the intercepts, which supports the decision to not include Acres as a slope predictor.

Longitudinal Data as Hierarchical: Time Nested Within Person

When we think of multilevel models, it is not unusual to think first of individual objects nested within a physical or social context, such as persons in neighborhoods, or hospitals in HMOs (see Table 1.2). However, as we saw earlier when we used GHLM to model votes on individual bills, multilevel modeling can be applied to multiple observations nested within a single object. This opens up multilevel modeling to a wide variety of useful applications. In particular, multilevel modeling can be applied to longitudinal

63

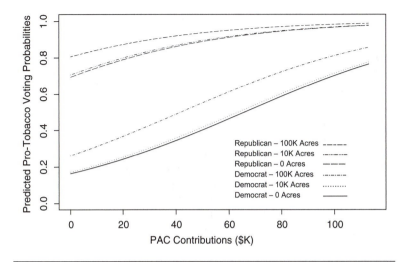

Figure 3.3   Predicted 3-level GHLM Binary Model Voting Probabilities

Months

Subject	1	2	3	4	5	6	7	8	9	10	11	12	13	14	15	16	17	18	19	20	21	22	23	24	25
001	X						X						X						X						X
002	X						X						X												
003	X						X																		X
004	X													X											
005	X					X															X			X	
006						X																		X	

Figure 3.4   A "Messy" Longitudinal Data Set

data where the primary interest is in modeling the structure and predictors of change over time.

Multilevel modeling has a number of important advantages when applied to longitudinal data compared to traditional analytic methods. Consider Figure 3.4, which illustrates different types of "messy" longitudinal data that may appear in a typical longitudinal study. Subject 001 represents the ideal situation where a participant is enrolled, given a baseline interview within the first month, and then is given four follow-up interviews every six months thereafter. Subject 002 is an example of somebody who drops out of the study or is lost to follow-up. Subject 003 has missing data for one or more

64

TABLE 3.4
LSOA Level-1 Data

CASEID	NUMADL	MARRIED	WAVE	WAVE2	IND1	IND2	IND3	IND4
1	0	No	.00	.00	1.00	.00	.00	.00
2	0	No	.00	.00	1.00	.00	.00	.00
2	0	No	1.00	1.00	.00	1.00	.00	.00
2	0	No	2.00	4.00	.00	.00	1.00	.00
2	1	No	3.00	9.00	.00	.00	.00	1.00
3	0	No	.00	.00	1.00	.00	.00	.00
3	0	No	3.00	9.00	.00	.00	.00	1.00
4	0	No	.00	.00	1.00	.00	.00	.00
4	5	No	1.00	1.00	.00	1.00	.00	.00
4	0	No	2.00	4.00	.00	.00	1.00	.00
4	1	No	3.00	9.00	.00	.00	.00	1.00

time points. Subject 004 has only one time point with valid data. Subject 005 has complete data for the baseline and four follow-up interviews, but the interviews occur either earlier or later than planned. Finally, Subject 006 has missing data *and* uneven time points.

Many traditional longitudinal approaches, such as repeated-measures MANOVA, are unable to easily handle longitudinal data that are unbalanced, have missing data, or have uneven time points. Multilevel modeling, on the other hand, is much more flexible and efficient. It will use whatever data are available, and it can model change patterns even for data that are collected at varying time points.

To illustrate a multilevel model of longitudinal data, we will use data taken from the Longitudinal Study of Aging (LSOA), which is a national biennial panel study of persons people 70 years or older undertaken from 1984 to 1990 by the National Center for Health Statistics (NCHS) in collaboration with the National Institute on Aging (NIA). The data used here were extracted from public-use data files available at ICPSR (http://webapp .icpsr.umich.edu/cocoon/ICPSR=STUDY/08719.xml). One of the major goals of the LSOA was to measure change in the functional status and living arrangements of older people, which makes it an ideal candidate for multilevel modeling. Participants who were at least 70 years old were enrolled and interviewed in 1984, and then re-interviewed every two years until 1990.

Tables 3.4 and 3.5 show the structure of the data files and variables used in this example, as required by HLM. The first table shows the

TABLE 3.5
LSOA Level-2 Data

CASEID	MALE	AGE84
1	Female	70
2	Male	87
3	Female	71
4	Male	78

interview-level (level-1) data set. Case ID is the participant ID and links the two data sets. NumADL is the number of types of activities of daily living with which the participant was having difficulties. This number could range from 0 to 7 and covered problems with bathing or showering, dressing, eating, getting in or out of bed or chair, walking, getting outside, and using or getting to the toilet. NumADL thus can be interpreted as a measure of functional status, with higher scores indicating lower functioning. Married is a binary variable that records whether the participant was married at the time of the interview. Because marital status can change, Married is considered to be a time-varying covariate and is included in the interview-level data set, not the participant-level data set. Wave is our time variable and indicates which interview is being done. It will be used to model linear change in NumADL. It has been reparameterized by subtracting 1, so the first interview is at Wave = 0. Wave^2 is the square of Wave, and will be used to test for quadratic change. IND1 to IND4 are four indicator variables that are used by the HLM software to designate the appropriate interview time point (other software such as SAS *PROC Mixed* or S-Plus *nlme* do not require the user to create these indicator variables).

The participant-level (level-2) data file is simpler, as shown in Table 3.5. Age84 is the age of the participant at the beginning of the study, and Male is a binary variable indicating the gender of the participant. Only covariates that are fixed across all time points are included in the person-level data set.

Our primary purpose in this example will be to model the trajectory of problems of daily living over a 6-year period. We will also be interested in how age, gender, and marital status influence these trajectories. The data used here include 20,283 interviews of 7,417 different participants. This is an average of 2.73 interviews per person. Given that every participant could have been interviewed four times, there is almost 32% "missing" data. In

66

TABLE 3.6
Sample Means of Number of ADLs Over Time

	Baseline	2 Years	4 Years	6 Years
Average number of problems in Activities of Daily Living (ADLs)	0.72	1.21	1.19	1.32

fact, only 2,330 participants (31.4%) have all four interviews. In other words, it would not be advisable to use repeated-measures ANOVA on these data; multilevel modeling, on the other hand, will be able to analyze all the data without losing any cases or information.

Table 3.6 presents the sample means of NumADL for each of the four surveys. Based on these sample means, it appears that functioning is decreasing over time; so, the first model to be fit will examine the linear and quadratic change over time in functioning, as well as the effects of age and gender:

Equation 3.10

$$\text{Level 1: } Y_{ij} = \beta_{0j} + \beta_{1j}(\text{Wave})_{ij} + \beta_{2j}(\text{Wave}^2)_{ij} + r_{ij}$$
$$\text{Level 2: } \beta_{0j} = \gamma_{00} + \gamma_{01}(\text{Male})_j + \gamma_{02}(\text{Age} - \overline{\text{Age}})_j + u_{0j}$$
$$\beta_{1j} = \gamma_{10} + u_{1j}$$
$$\beta_{2j} = \gamma_{20} + u_{2j}$$

Notice that we are allowing the time slopes (β_1 and β_2) to vary between persons but we are not trying to model that variation with person-level predictors. Also, we have centered the person-level predictor Age by subtracting its grand mean. If we had not centered Age, then we would have to interpret the intercept as applying to a person who was 0 years old.

The results of this first model (Model 1) are displayed on the left side of Table 3.7. Prediction profiles based on these results are presented in Figure 3.5, for persons who were of average age for the study (76.8 years) in 1984. Both men and women started the study averaging less than one ADL. This increases steadily over the next 6 years. The parameter estimate of .473 for Wave indicates a steady linear increase of about half

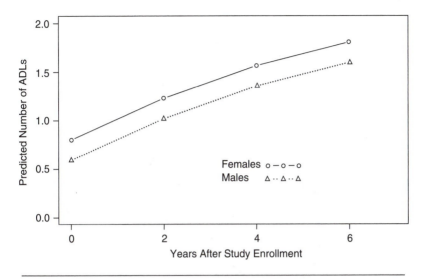

Figure 3.5   Predicted ADL Trajectories Over Time by Gender

of an ADL every two years. Although significant, the coefficient of $-.046$ for Wave[2] is an order of magnitude smaller than that of the linear effect. This quadratic effect can be crudely interpreted as the rate of change— as time passes, the decrease in functioning level is slowing down. Men function slightly better than women ($-.210$), and every year of increased age is associated with a .073 increase in number of ADLs.

The estimates of the variability of the random effects show that there is approximately the same intra-individual variability (1.014) as inter-individual variability (1.070). Given the size of the fixed effects, this suggests that there is still substantial unmodeled variability left.

Models 2 and 3 in Table 3.7 are elaborations of our first model. Model 2 adds the level-1 time-varying predictor Married (Equation 3.11). This tests the hypothesis that people who are married at the time of their interview have better functioning than those who are not married. Married is entered as a fixed effect because HLM would not converge otherwise. This may be due to lack of variability of Married within and across persons. The results, however, show that marital status is not a significant predictor of functioning.

TABLE 3.7

Parameter Estimates and Model Fit for LSOA Longitudinal Analyses

Fixed Effects	Model 1				Model 2				Model 3			
	Coef.	SE	T-ratio	p	Coef.	SE	T-ratio	p	Coef.	SE	T-ratio	p
For Intercept (β_{0j})												
Intercept (γ_{00})	.802	.021	37.4	.000	.818	.024	34.3	.000	.816	.024	34.0	.000
Male (γ_{01})	−.210	.034	6.1	.000	−.189	.037	5.1	.000	−.185	.038	4.87	.000
Age (γ_{02})	.073	.003	24.5	.000	.072	.003	23.6	.000	.003	.003	23.6	.000
For Wave Slope (β_{1j})												
Wave (γ_{10})	.473	.025	19.0	.000	.472	.025	18.9	.000	.470	.031	15.1	.000
Male (γ_{11})									.006	.052	0.1	.900
For Wave^2 Slope (β_{2j})												
Wave^2 (γ_{20})	−.046	.008	5.4	.000	−.046	.008	5.4	.000	−.043	.010	4.13	.000
Male (γ_{21})									−.007	.018	0.4	.679
For Married Slope (β_{3j})												
Married (γ_{30})					−.051	.033	1.5	.128	−.051	.033	1.5	.130

(Continued)

TABLE 3.7
(Continued)

Random Effects	Model 1		Model 2		Model 3	
	Std. Dev.	Var. Comp.	Std. Dev.	Var. Comp.	Std. Dev.	Var. Comp.
Intercept (u_{0j})	1.070	1.144	1.070	1.144	1.070	1.144
Wave Slope (u_{1j})	.704	.495	.703	.494	.703	.494
Wave^2 Slope (u_{2j})	.195	.038	.195	.038	.195	.038
Level-1 (r_{ij})	1.014	1.029	1.014	1.029	1.014	1.029

Model Fit	Deviance	Parameters	AIC	BIC	Deviance	Parameters	AIC	BIC	Deviance	Parameters	AIC	BIC
	73967	12	73991	74074	73965	13	73991	74081	73964	15	73994	74098

69

Equation 3.11

Level 1: $Y_{ij} = \beta_{0j} + \beta_{1j}(\text{Wave})_{ij} + \beta_{2j}(\text{Wave}^2)_{ij} + \beta_{3j}(\text{Married})_{ij} + r_{ij}$

Level 2: $\beta_{0j} = \gamma_{00} + \gamma_{01}(\text{Male})_j + \gamma_{02}(\text{Age} - \overline{\text{Age}})_j + u_{0j}$

$\beta_{1j} = \gamma_{10} + u_{1j}$

$\beta_{2j} = \gamma_{20} + u_{2j}$

$\beta_{3j} = \gamma_{30}$

Model 1 includes gender only as a main effect. We can easily check to see if men and women have the same functioning trajectories by including cross-level interactions in the model. These interactions have been included in Model 3 (Equation 3.12). The results show that there is not a gender by linear, or a gender by quadratic interaction.

Equation 3.12

Level 1: $Y_{ij} = \beta_{0j} + \beta_{1j}(\text{Wave})_{ij} + \beta_{2j}(\text{Wave}^2)_{ij} + \beta_{3j}(\text{Married})_{ij} + r_{ij}$

Level 2: $\beta_{0j} = \gamma_{00} + \gamma_{01}(\text{Male})_j + \gamma_{02}(\text{Age} - \overline{\text{Age}})_j + u_{0j}$

$\beta_{1j} = \gamma_{10} + \gamma_{11}(\text{Male})_j + u_{1j}$

$\beta_{2j} = \gamma_{20} + \gamma_{21}(\text{Male})_j + u_{2j}$

$\beta_{3j} = \gamma_{30}$

The individual coefficient statistics suggest that there is no reason to prefer Models 2 or 3 over Model 1. Of the three overall model fit statistics, the BIC is most successful at separating the models. This will often be the case for large samples, because the BIC takes sample size into account when penalizing the deviance. The smallest BIC is for Model 1, also indicating that it is the best model.

Many of these model-building steps for longitudinal data are the same as those we have used in the previous multilevel models. However, there is one additional consideration that is important for the analyst to consider when dealing with longitudinal models. In non-longitudinal models, we typically assume that errors are normally distributed and independent. This independence assumption is often not appropriate for longitudinal data. Therefore, the analyst will generally need to choose an appropriate alternative error covariance structure for the longitudinal data. Most multilevel modeling software will allow specification of alternative covariance structures, although they vary in user-friendliness.

TABLE 3.8
LSOA Model 1 Fit With Different Error Covariance Structures

Name	Parameters	Deviance	AIC	BIC
Unrestricted (unstructured)	15	73879	73909	74013
Homogeneous (compound symmetry)	12	73967	73991	74074
Autoregressive	13	74340	74366	74456

Table 3.8 shows the fit indexes for Model 1 with three different covariance structures. The most general type of error structure, called *unrestricted* or sometimes *unstructured,* makes no assumptions about the error terms, and allows for any pattern of correlated errors across occasions. An unrestricted covariance structure will always have the highest number of random parameters, because every lag will have its own separate covariance estimated from the data. So, although the deviance for an unrestricted error model will always be the lowest, it will also be the least parsimonious model under consideration. Other, more restricted error structures are usually more theoretically justifiable, and simpler to estimate. Therefore, the unrestricted model often acts as a baseline model against which other models are compared.

Instead of allowing all of the covariances to vary freely, you can assume that the covariances are constant across all occasions, or, equivalently, that there is a single value for all correlations between time points. This much more restrictive assumption is called *homogeneous error.* This error structure is the same as the *compound symmetry* assumption that underlies repeated-measures univariate ANOVA. This assumption is attractive because of its parsimony, and this model will usually have the smallest number of parameters. However, compound symmetry is a restrictive assumption that is not usually met by real-world data.

An alternative error structure that is often used for longitudinal data is that of *autoregressive* structure, also sometimes called first-order autoregressive. This error structure lies between a fully unrestricted error structure and the highly restrictive homogeneous error. An autoregressive covariance structure assumes that error terms are correlated across first-order lags. So, if the lag correlation is estimated at .30, this means that errors at Time 1 and Time 2 are correlated at .30, Time 2 and Time 3 at .30, and so on. The implication of this is that larger lags have smaller correlations: The errors at Time 1 and Time 3 will be correlated less than .30. The autoregressive structure is almost as parsimonious as homogeneous error; only one more parameter needs to be estimated: *rho*, which is the first-order correlation. The model fit indexes in Table 3.8 show that for the LSOA model, the autoregressive error structure provides the worst fit to the data. The unrestricted and homogeneous structures seem to be comparable. Therefore, for reasons of parsimony, we would choose the homogeneous error covariance structure for these data and this model. (In fact, the results presented in Table 3.7 are using the homogeneous error structure.) One reason that there is little difference between these two error structures is that we have only four time points. As the number of time points increases, the number of parameters for the unrestricted model will increase dramatically, and we would expect to see bigger differences between the various error structure choices.

This section just touches on the most important topics of using multilevel models with longitudinal data. For more details on such issues as additional error covariance structures, how to model non-linear and discontinuous change, the relationship to time-series analysis, and software issues, the reader should seek out one of these excellent advanced volumes: Little, Schnabel, and Baumert (2000); Moskowitz and Hershberger (2002); or Singer and Willett (2003).

APPENDICES

Data Sets and Other Support Materials

The two data sets used throughout this book are available online at the author's website: http://biostats.slu.edu/multimodel.htm. In addition to the data, all of the HLM and R/S-Plus programs that were used to analyze the data and produce the statistical and graphical output are available. A list of multilevel modeling resources is also regularly maintained there.

Software

The focus of this book has been to present a conceptual and statistical introduction to multilevel modeling techniques. Although the examples have used two common statistical packages (HLM and R/S-Plus), a detailed discussion of how to choose and use any particular multilevel modeling software package is beyond the scope of this book. In addition, any in-depth software review would be out of date within the first few months after publication. That being said, deciding what software to use can be a daunting task. Different programs take very different approaches to multilevel modeling, each package has its own strengths and weaknesses, and some of the software can be quite expensive. Here are a few suggestions that may help in choosing the right package.

Table A.1 lists some basic information about the most commonly used multilevel modeling software. One of the first choices confronting a novice multilevel analyst is whether to use a specialized multilevel package (e.g., HLM or MLwiN), or to use the mixed-effects procedures that exist within general purpose statistics software (e.g., the mixed procedures in SAS and SPSS, or the *lme* and *nlme* procedures in R/S-Plus.). The main advantage of using SAS, SPSS, or R is that the user probably already owns this software and knows how to use it. However, in general, there is less documentation available on how to use these packages specifically for multilevel modeling. Also, the big three packages all use a mixed-effects modeling approach that can be confusing to use, especially for complicated models (such as 3-level models).

HLM and MLwiN are both sophisticated programs that can estimate complex multilevel models. Their documentation is quite good; MLwiN in particular has an excellent set of tutorials. These programs generally have fewer modeling limitations than the general purpose software. They also tend to have fewer problems with model convergence and estimate models more quickly. (SAS, in particular, can be extremely slow at estimating complex models.) Because HLM and MLwiN are specialized programs, they are more limited in their data management and graphical analysis capabilities.

For all of these reasons, if you are going to be doing extensive multilevel modeling, it is probably worthwhile to at least try out HLM or MLwiN. Both of these products have demo versions available at their main support Web sites. This short discussion has focused only on the major packages; however, there are numerous other software programs that can be used for many types of multilevel modeling. See the resources listed below for more information. For more detailed comparisons of multilevel modeling software, see de Leeuw and Kreft (2001).

TABLE A.1
Information About Multilevel Modeling Software

Specialized Multilevel Modeling Software

	Version	Stat. Model	Levels	GHLM	Interface	Website	Core References
HLM	5.04	Multilevel	3	Yes	Graphical	http://www.ssicentral.com/hlm/hlm.htm	Raudenbush et al. (2000)
MLwiN	2.0 (Beta)	Multilevel	3+	Yes	Graphical	http://multilevel.ioe.ac.uk	Rasbash et al. (2000)

General Purpose Software

	Version	Stat. Model	Levels	GHLM	Interface	Website	Core References
R/S-Plus–nlme or lme	Lme4 0.4–4	Mixed	3	Yes	Syntax	http://cran.r-project.org http://nlme.stat.wisc.edu/	Pinheiro and Bates (2000)
SAS-Proc Mixed	8.2	Mixed	3	Yes	Syntax	http://www.sas.com	Littell et al. (1996) Singer (1998)
SPSS – MIXED	12.0	Mixed	3	No	Either	http://www.spss.com	SPSS Advanced Models documentation

Other Resources

There are numerous resources are available to help the newcomer learn multilevel modeling techniques, as well as to help more experienced analysts deal with complicated multilevel modeling situations. One of the best all-purpose multilevel modeling Web sites is maintained by the Center for Multilevel Modeling, at http://multilevel.ioe.ac.uk/. In addition to being the main support Web site for MLwiN, it contains a very good multilevel modeling bibliography, and a collection of multilevel modeling software reviews.

UCLA maintains an extensive multilevel modeling Web portal at http://statcomp.ats.ucla.edu/mlm/. It acts as an easy- to- use search engine for all things related to multilevel modeling. One particularly useful resource here is a set of data and programming examples to accompany Singer and Willet's *Applied Longitudinal Data Analysis* (http://www.ats.ucla.edu/stat/mlwin/examples/alda/default.htm). Here, you can compare how the same multilevel analyses are run for various software packages, including all of the packages reviewed above.

Finally, anybody who plans to use multilevel techniques regularly will benefit from subscribing to the Multilevel Modeling Discussion List. Multilevel modeling researchers and software developers regularly participate in this email list. You can subscribe to the list and view the list archives at http://www.jiscmail.ac.uk/lists/multilevel.html.

REFERENCES

Akaike, H. (1987). Factor analysis and the AIC. *Psychometrika, 52,* 317–332.

Armitage, P., & Colton, T. (1998). *Encyclopedia of biostatistics.* New York: J. Wiley.

Becker, R. A., & Cleveland, W. S. (1996). *S-Plus Trellis Graphics user's manual.* Seattle: MathSoft, Inc.

Bhaskar, R. (1989). *The possibility of naturalism: A philosophical critique of the contemporary human sciences.* Atlantic Highlands, New Jersey: Humanities Press.

Boyle, M. H., & Willms, J. D. (2001). Multilevel modeling of hierarchical data in developmental studies. *Journal of Child Psychology and Psychiatry, 42,* 141–162.

Buka, S. L., Brennan, R. T., Rich-Edwards, J. W., Raudenbush, S. W., & Earls, F. (2003). Neighborhood support and the birth weight of urban infants. *American Journal of Epidemiology, 157,* 1–8.

Carroll, K. (1975). Experimental evidence of dietary factors and hormone-dependent cancers. *Cancer Research, 35,* 3374–3383.

Cleveland, W. S. (1993). *Visualizing data.* Summit, New Jersey: Hobart Press.

76

Curran, P. J., Stice, E., & Chassin, L. (1997). The relation between adolescent and peer alcohol use: A longitudinal random coefficients model. *Journal of Consulting and Clinical Psychology, 65,* 130–140.

de Leeuw, J., & Kreft, I.G.G. (2001). Software for multilevel analysis. In A. H. Leyland & H. Goldstein (Eds.), *Multilevel modelling of health statistics* (pp. 187–204). Chichester, UK: Wiley. Available online at: http://preprints.stat.ucla.edu/239/239.pdf

Diez-Roux, A. V., Merkin, S. S., Arnett, D., aet al. (2001). Neighborhood of residence and incidence of coronary heart disease. *New England Journal of Medicine, 345,* 99–106.

Duncan, C., Jones, K., & Moon, G. (1998). Context, composition and heterogeneity: Using multilevel models in health research. *Social Science and Medicine, 46,* 97–117.

Freedman, D. A. (2001). Ecological inference and the ecological fallacy. In N. J. Smelser & P. B. Baltes (Eds.), *International encyclopedia of the social & behavioral sciences.* Vol. 6, pp. 4027–4030. New York: Elsevier.

Gebbie, K., Rosenstock, L., & Hernandez, L. M. (2003). *Who will keep the public healthy? Educating public health professionals for the 21st century.* Washington, D.C.: The National Academies Press.

Goldstein, H., Yang, M., Omar, R., Turner, R., & Thompson, S. (2000). Meta-analysis using multilevel models with an application to the study of class size effects. *Applied Statistics, 49,* 399–412.

Harrell, F. E. (2001). *Regression modeling strategies: With applications to linear models, logistic regression, and survival analysis.* New York: Springer.

Heck, R. H., & Thomas, S. L. (2000). *An introduction to multilevel modeling techniques.* Mahwah, NJ: Lawrence Erlbaum Associates.

Holmes, M. D., Hunter, D. J., Colditz, G. A., Stampfer, M. J., Hankinson, S. E., Speizer, F. E., Rosner, B., & Willett, W. C. (1999). Association of dietary intake of fat and fatty acids with risk of breast cancer. *Journal of the American Medical Association, 281,* 914–920.

Hox, J. (2002). *Multilevel analysis.* Mahwah, NJ: Lawrence Erlbaum Associates.

Kreft, I. (1995). The effects of centering in multilevel analysis: Is the public school the loser or the winner? A new analysis of an old question. *Multilevel Modelling Newsletter, 7,* 5–8. Available online at: http://multilevel.ioe.ac.uk/publref/newsletters.html.

Kreft, I., & de Leeuw, J. (1998). *Introducing multilevel modeling.* London: Sage Publications.

Lazarsfeld, P. F., & Menzel, H. (1969). On the relation between individual and collective properties. In A. Etzioni (Ed.), *A sociological reader on complex organizations* (pp. 499–516). New York: Holt, Rinehart, and Winston.

Leyland, A. H., & Goldstein, H. (2001). *Multilevel modeling of health statistics.* Chicester, UK: John Wiley & Sons.

Littell, R. C., Milliken, G. A., Stroup, W. W., & Wolfinger, R. S. (1996). *SAS system for mixed models.* Cary, NC: SAS Institute Inc.

Little, T. D., Schnabel, K. U., & Baumert, J. (2000). *Modeling longitudinal and multilevel data: Practical issues, applied approaches and specific examples.* Mahwah, NJ: Lawrence Erlbaum Associates.

Lochner, K., Pamuk, E., Makuc, D., Kennedy, B. P., & Kawachi, I. (2001). State-level income inequality and individual mortality risk: A prospective, multilevel study. *American Journal of Public Health, 91,* 385–391.

Longford, N. T. (1989). To center or not to center. *Multilevel Modelling Newsletter, 1,* 7, 11. Available online at: http://multilevel.ioe.ac.uk/publref/newsletters.html.

Longford, N. T. (1993). *Random coefficient models.* New York: Oxford University Press.

Luke, D. A., & Krauss, M. (2004, under review). The influence of tobacco industry PAC contributions on voting behavior in the U.S. Congress.

Maes, L., & Lievens, J. (2003). Can the school make a difference? A multilevel analysis of adolescent risk and health behaviour. *Social Science & Medicine, 56*, 517–529.

McArdle, J. J., & Epstein, D. (1987). Latent growth curves within developmental structural equation models. *Child Development, 58*, 110–133.

Moos, R. H. (1996). Understanding environments: The key to improving social processes and program outcomes. *American Journal of Community Psychology, 24*, 193–201.

Moskowitz, D. S., & Hershberger, S. L. (Eds.). (2002). *Modeling intraindividual variability with repeated measures data: Applications and techniques.* Hillsdale, NJ: Lawrence Erlbaum Associates.

Mossholder, K. W., Bennett, N., & Martin, C. L. (1998). A multilevel analysis of procedural justice context. *Journal of Organizational Behavior, 19*, 131–141.

Muthén, B. O. (1994). Multilevel covariance structure analysis. *Sociological Methods & Research, 22*, 376–398.

O'Brien, R. M. (2000). Levels of analysis. In E. G. Borgbatta and & R. Montgomery (Eds.), *Encyclopedia of sociology,* (2nd ed., (pp. 1591–1596). New York: Macmillan.

Office of Behavioral and Social Sciences Research. (2000). *Toward higher levels of analysis: Progress and promise in research on social and cultural dimensions of health* (NIH Publication No. 01–5020). Bethesda, MD: National Institutes of Health. Available online at: http://obssr.od.nih.gov/Conf_Wkshp/higherlevel/conference.html.

Perkins, D. D., Wandersman, A., Rich, R. C., & Taylor, R. B. (1993). The physical environment of street crime: Defensible space, territoriality and incivilities. *Journal of Environmental Psychology, 13*, 29–49.

Pinheiro, J. C., & Bates, D. M. (2000). *Mixed-effects models in S and S-Plus.* New York: Springer.

Pinheiro, J. C., Bates, D. M., DebRoy, S., & Sarkar, D. (2003). *The nlme package.* Available online at: http://cran.r-project.org/doc/packages/nlme.pdf.

Plewis, I. (1989). Comment on "Centering predictors in multilevel analysis." *Multilevel Modelling Newsletter, 1*, 6, 11. Available online at: http://multilevel.ioe.ac.uk/publref/newsletters.html.

Rasbash, J., Browne, W., Goldstein, H., Yang, M., Plewis, I., Healy, M., Woodhouse, G., Draper, D., Langford, I., & Lewis, T. (2000). *A user's guide to MLwiN* (Version 2.1b). London: University of London, Institute of Education.

Raudenbush, S. W. (1989). "Centering" predictors in multilevel analysis: Choices and consequences. *Multilevel Modelling Newsletter, 1*, 10–12. Available online at: http://multilevel.ioe.ac.uk/publref/newsletters.html.

Raudenbush, S. W., & Bryk, A. S. (1985). Empirical Bayes meta-analysis. *Journal of Educational Statistics, 10*, 75–98.

Raudenbush, S. W., & Bryk, A. S. (2002). *Hierarchical linear models: Applications and data analysis methods* (2nd. ed.).Thousand Oaks, CA: Sage Publications.

Raudenbush, S. W., Bryk, A. S., Cheong, Y. F., & Congdon, R. (2000). *HLM 5: Hierarchical linear and nonlinear modeling.* Lincolnwood, IL: SSI Scientific Software International.

Rice, N., Carr-Hill, R., Dixon, P., & Sutton, M. (1998). The influence of households on drinking behaviour: A multilevel analysis. *Social Science & Medicine, 46*, 971–979.

Schwarz, G. (1978). Estimating the dimension of a model. *Annals of Statistics, 6*, 461–464.

78

Shinn, M., & Rapkin, B. D. (2000). Cross-level research without cross-ups in community psychology. In J. Rappaport & E. Seidman (Eds.), *Handbook of community psychology*, (pp. 669–695). New York: Kluwer Academic/Plenum Publishers.

Singer, J. D. (1998). Using SAS PROC MIXED to fit multilevel models, hierarchical models, and individual growth models. *Journal of Educational and Behavioral Statistics, 24,* 323–355.

Singer, J. D., & Willett, J. B. (2003). *Applied longitudinal data analysis: Modeling change and event occurrence.* New York: Oxford University Press.

Snijders, T., & Bosker, R. (1994). Modeled variance in two-level models. *Sociological Methods & Research, 22,* 342–363.

Snijders, T., & Bosker, R. (1999). *Multilevel analysis: An introduction to basic and advanced multilevel modeling.* London: Sage Publications.

Villemez, W. J., & Bridges, W. P. (1988). When bigger is better: Differences in the individual-level effect of firm and establishment size. *American Sociological Review, 53,* 237–255.

ABOUT THE AUTHOR

Douglas A. Luke is currently an associate professor of community health at Saint Louis University, School of Public Health, where he is serving as chair of the biostatistics division. In 1990, he received his Ph.D. in clinical/community psychology with a minor in quantitative psychology from the University of Illinois. While at the University of Illinois, he studied under a number of notable quantitative scientists and authors, including Phipps Arabie (co-author of *Three-Way Scaling and Clustering*), Stanley Wasserman (editor of *Advances in Social Network Analysis*), Larry Jones, Larry Hubert, and Ledyard Tucker. His 1991 article, "Expanding Behavior Setting Theory: Setting Phenotypes in a Mutual Help Organization," was recently selected as one of the ten most influential methodology articles published in the first 25 years of the *American Journal of Psychology*. In addition to multilevel modeling, his major areas of quantitative interest include cluster analysis, network analysis, survival analysis, and geographic information systems (GIS). His substantive interests include tobacco control evaluation and policy and media policy related to health behavior.